SLOW DEATH

SLOW DEATH
MEMOIRS OF A CRICKET UMPIRE

Rudi Koertzen
with Chris Schoeman

Published by Zebra Press
an imprint of Random House Struik (Pty) Ltd
Reg. No. 1966/003153/07
80 McKenzie Street, Cape Town, 8001
PO Box 1144, Cape Town, 8000 South Africa

www.zebrapress.co.za

First published 2010

1 3 5 7 9 10 8 6 4 2

Publication © Zebra Press 2010
Text © Rudi Koertzen and Chris Schoeman 2010

Cover photographs © *The Times*, 3 August 2009/nisyndication.com (front);
iStockphoto (back)

PUBLISHER: Marlene Fryer
MANAGING EDITOR: Robert Plummer
EDITOR: Ronel Richter-Herbert
COVER DESIGNER: Sean Robertson
TEXT DESIGNER: Monique Oberholzer
TYPESETTER: Monique van den Berg
INDEXER: Fiona Potter
PRODUCTION MANAGER: Valerie Kömmer

Set in 11.5 pt on 15 pt Adobe Garamond

Printed and bound by Interpak Books, Pietermaritzburg

ISBN 978 1 77022 079 9

Over 50 000 unique African images available to purchase
from our image bank at www.imagesofafrica.co.za

To my wife Hyla and my children
Yulali, Eumelda, Rudolf and Luan

Contents

Foreword

When I appeared on the South African cricket scene as a young-ster for Western Province back in 1993/94, Rudi Koertzen had been plying his trade as first-class umpire for 10 years already. Since then our paths have crossed regularly on the cricket field on both the provincial and international scene, and after all these years, Rudi is still at the very top of his career. The agonisingly slow raising of his left finger when 'Slow Death' sends players back to the pavilion has become one of the most familiar – and dreaded! – sights in international cricket.

Over the years I have grown to like and respect Rudi both as a person and as an umpire. For umpires, as for players, you have to be the best to survive at the top. And if it is difficult to get to the top, it is even harder to stay there. Rudi is one of those who stood out all along. Players look for consistency in umpires, which they get with Rudi. Like all other umpires, Rudi has made some mis-takes in his time, but because of his dedication to be the best and the hard work he puts in, he counts among those who have made the fewest bad decisions. I, for one, feel reassured when I see Rudi at the crease.

From personal experience I know that he commands a lot of respect from players all around the world. On the field he goes about his job very professionally, but he remains an affable bloke who maintains good relations with the players. I know how much pressure the players try to put on umpires – they will try their luck, for sure. But Rudi doesn't allow the pressure to get to him. It's a trait that he has developed over many years of experience in the hot cauldron of international cricket.

No other umpire in the world has achieved what Rudi has – standing in more than 100 Tests and more than 200 One Day Internationals. It couldn't have happened to a nicer guy. The one thing I have always admired about Rudi, apart from his on-field umpiring ability, is the incredible passion he feels for the game. He absolutely loves cricket. There are, in fact, some players who could do with his kind of dedication.

From a player's perspective, I have to say I've never envied Rudi and the other umpires their job. They stand out there for hours, for days in a row, having to make crucial decisions all the time, and coping with all kinds of pressure and criticism from the players, the media and the public. Over the past few years television technology has played a positive role in assisting umpires in their decision-making, but I wouldn't like to see every decision taken away from them. We still want a human element as part of the umpiring scene; we don't want them to become robots.

Thanks, Rudi, for what you have given to cricket over such a long period of time. The way you have lived your love for the game has been an example and inspiration to all involved in the sport. It is indeed a privilege to have written a foreword to your autobiography. I know that one day you will hang up your white coat, but your passion for the bat and the ball will live on.

JACQUES KALLIS

Author's note

Apart from his great passion for cricket, I will always remember Rudi for a question he asked one bright Eastern Cape morning of our Sunday-school teacher, a bloke with the nickname Vonk (Spark), derived from his flaming-red hair and his love of fast motorbikes and cars. We were still skinny, knobbly-kneed little brats in primary school. 'Tell me, sir,' Rudi asked, 'how does it work that only 144 000 people will go to heaven, as it says in the Bible?' For a moment we thought Rudi had bowled him a googly, but Vonk quickly responded, 'Now don't you worry about that, *boet*; you just make sure you're one of them.'

One could joke about it and say that the way umpires have cheated batsmen out of runs before the use of technology, Rudi doesn't stand much of a chance! But I have to say, should it depend on one's love for cricket, he would be in the front of the line.

I've been fortunate to have known Rudi since our primary-school days, when as kids we walked the dirt roads of our town and played many cricket games together. So I know exactly where he's come from. After school our ways parted, and years later I started reading about him as a provincial umpire and eventually a Test umpire. At school he'd always been a gutsy little bugger, so I was not surprised that he had risen to those heights. Since then I have watched him on television, umpiring in all corners of the world.

With the exceptional milestones of 100 Tests and 200 One Day Internationals approaching, I thought that his career surely deserved to be immortalised in book form, and I'm grateful to Zebra Press for supporting the idea.

All I can say is: Well done, Rudi, for your wonderful achievements in international cricket. And thanks for sharing your career with me while we worked on this book. I am privileged to have been involved in this way.

CHRIS SCHOEMAN

Abbreviations

ANC: African National Congress

BBC: British Broadcasting Corporation

BCCI: Board of Control for Cricket in India

CEO: chief executive officer

D/L: Duckworth-Lewis (method)

DRS: decision review system

FICA: Federation of International Cricketers' Associations

FIFA: International Federation of Association Football

ICC: International Cricket Council

ICL: Indian Cricket League

IPL: Indian Premier League

MCC: Marylebone Cricket Club

MCG: Melbourne Cricket Ground

ODI: One Day International

PCB: Pakistan Cricket Board

PSS: Pakiosothy Saravanamuttu Stadium

QC: Queen's Counsel

SABC: South African Broadcasting Corporation

SCG: Sydney Cricket Ground

SSC: Sinhalese Sports Club

T20: Twenty20

UCBSA: United Cricket Board of South Africa

UPMs: umpires' performance managers

WACA: Western Australian Cricket Association

WICB: West Indies Cricket Board

Introduction

When I started umpiring in 1981, I did it just so that I could be involved with the game that I love. I never dreamt that I would one day be standing on the international stage. As South Africa was barred from international competition at the time, such a thought was far from my mind. But thanks to the country's return to international cricket in 1991, I was given a chance to progress up the ladder of provincial and, eventually, international umpiring.

I have always been a stickler for setting myself goals, and fortunately my longevity in the game enabled me to reach a few significant milestones. When I entered the international ranks, I thought that standing in even 50 One Day Internationals would be quite something. But 50 ODIs came and went, so next I targeted 100 ODIs. In the meantime I was also given the opportunity to stand in more and more Tests, which are, in the final analysis, the benchmark for one's umpiring abilities, and the number of Tests in which I officiated also grew steadily. And so it went on. Today I am very happy with and content in the knowledge that I have stood in 100 Tests and 200 ODIs – a milestone no one had achieved before me. To date, I'm also the only international umpire to have stood in 200 ODIs.

For someone who started international umpiring relatively late in life, these milestones have been a huge personal achievement and a wonderful dream come true. The only objective that has passed me by all these years was standing in an ICC (International Cricket Council) World Cup final. I was third umpire in 2003 in South Africa and in 2007 in the West Indies. But with the next World Cup only due in 2011, and my retirement imminent, standing in the final may forever remain an unaccomplished goal.

I can ascribe my achievements, such as they are, to my passion for this great game, and – without trying to blow my own trumpet – to dedication and fitness. At the time of achieving my double of 100 Tests and 200 ODIs, the ICC congratulated me for serving the game through my umpiring and for being a role model for and inspiration to young up-and-coming umpires. I sincerely hope that I have achieved the latter.

The job of umpiring has its highs and lows, but I can assure you that the highs far outweigh the lows. Over the years I have officiated on all the big continents of the globe, from the grounds in my home country of South Africa to the colourful, festive grounds of the Caribbean and the graceful ambience of the hallowed ground at Lord's. Being an international cricket umpire has given me the opportunity to travel to a host of different countries, meet an interesting variety of people and learn about different cultures. Over a long period of time, I could also watch the young emerging cricketers of yesterday develop into the great stars of today. For that I will always be extremely grateful to the great game of cricket.

Yes, I've been fortunate to have had so many opportunities, but the real heroes in the story of my life have been my wife Hyla and our four children, Yalali, Eumelda, Rudolf and Luan. I haven't been able to spend too much time with them over the past 17 years because I have been away for so much of each year. I have been fully aware that my absence is a burden on them, but I will be forever grateful for the way they have shown understanding and allowed me to live one of the great passions of my life, which at the same time also happened to be my job.

This long cricketing life has enabled me to collect so many wonderful – and some not so wonderful – memories of players, matches and grounds all around the world, and I can now recount all those reminiscences within the pages of this book.

Every umpire has a trait that makes him unique, and so have I – a trait, in fact, that has given rise to the book's title: *Slow Death*. I have a slow and deliberate way of raising my left finger when giving batsmen out – I can just imagine how they must have dreaded that sign!

When I first started umpiring, I stood with my hands in front of my body, but it meant that every time I moved them after a delivery, batsmen got jumpy because they thought, 'Oh no, here it is,' thinking that I was going to lift my finger and give them out. That's when I decided to stand with my hands behind my back, and since then I have gripped my left wrist with my right hand, which helps to stop me from shooting up my left hand without thinking about a decision. That has become my trademark and has given rise to my nickname of Slow Death.

Traditional or 'real' umpiring to me is standing on-field, and although you can also see a lot from the stand as third or fourth umpire, you're really no more than just another spectator in the ground. But standing on the pitch, among the players … It lends a different dimension. You get all the vibes and sounds and talking first hand; it is simply the best seat in the whole ground. So, for the purposes of this book, I will largely stick to my on-field umpiring experiences, and only describe what I've seen from behind the stumps and from square leg. I hope you enjoy it as much as I did.

1

A Huckleberry Finn childhood

" *How I loved the sounds and smells of cricket as a youngster! The leather ball against willow, the sharp thud as the ball hit the boundary pickets, the firm but polite clapping of the spectators. And the smells – linseed oil on bats, brand-new leather balls and freshly mowed outfields.* "

I was born Rudolf Eric Koertzen in Knysna, South Africa, on 26 March 1949, the youngest of three children. My sister Marie is the oldest; then came my other sister, Fonnie, and then me. To put my birth in a South African perspective, I was born within a year of the National Party of Dr DF Malan coming to power after ousting General Jan Christiaan Smuts's United Party from government. At the time, Malan's party was, of course, propagating the policy of apartheid, which would cause the country so much trouble in the future, resulting in our cricket isolation for many years, among other things.

My father, Josef, grew up in the Mossel Bay area, while my mother, Maria, hailed from George, also in the Southern Cape. My father worked as a truck driver for the South African Railways and Harbours, a government department. He spent a lot of time on the road, sometimes only seeing his family over weekends. In those days loyalty to employers was a main priority, and most men used to stick with the same company for the whole of their working careers. For my father it was no different. He would work for the SA Railways all his life, and by the time I was born in Knysna, he had already been working for them for a fair number of years.

It was almost the norm for Railways employees to be transferred around the country, and from Knysna my father was transferred to Noupoort, a large, dusty railway junction in the Great Karoo. Noupoort was an old, established town; during the Anglo-Boer War, already, it had been used as a military base by the British forces in the Cape Colony. After a few years' service in Noupoort, my father was transferred to the Eastern Cape town of Despatch, and that's where I started my primary-school education at the age of six.

Before 1980, there weren't all that many people who would have been able to tell you exactly where in the country Despatch was situated. At that stage, some had not even heard of it. But then a brilliant rugby player called Danie Gerber put the town on the map. A product of the local Despatch High School, Danie became a Springbok in 1980 and went on to become a world legend.

I think the greatest compliment he was ever given was when the famous BBC commentator Bill McLaren named him as the best outside centre he had seen in his 50-odd years of rugby commentating. Under Danie's leadership, the local rugby club also won the national club championships twice in the 1980s, ahead of club giants like the universities of Stellenbosch and Pretoria.

In 1997, the local school produced another Springbok in Rassie Erasmus, who made his debut as a loose forward against Martin Johnson's British Lions. Rassie had vision; he was a rugby genius. Well, he still is. He retired as a player after 36 tests, and then – aged only 33 – coached the Free State Cheetahs to Currie

Cup victory in 2005. Since his move to Cape Town he has been coaching the Stormers in the Super 14 with a fair degree of success.

Internationally known jockey Michael (Muis) Roberts also had a brief stint in our primary school before his parents sent him off to a jockey academy in Port Elizabeth – with spectacular results. Then, of course, Brian Jerling, another current international cricket umpire, spent 15 years of his adult life in Despatch. Brian became a familiar face on local TV some years ago when he appeared in ads for cricket sponsors Toyota.

So you can be sure that, these days, when a man mentions the town's name through the foam of his beer, it's with some respect.

The early townsfolk never liked the Union Jack, but I guess in that Despatch wasn't much different from a lot of towns in the country – except those in Natal, of course! I recall that during the 1960s there was a suggestion that the town be renamed after the then prime minister, John Vorster, which caused quite a stir at the time. Vorster himself had no objection to the idea, but it could be done on one condition only, and that was that the townspeople's decision had to be unanimous. A meeting was held on the town's rugby field – a piece of land that in later years was to be graced by some of the big names in world rugby, as I mentioned – and every living soul was there. The proposed name change, however, died a quick death, as too many people were dead against it.

For as long as I could remember, the town's only hotel, an old building with gables and verandahs, had been there. Set among some big old eucalyptus trees, it was the popular place for sportsmen to quench their thirst, and because of the trees, was affectionately known as the 'Lang Bome' (tall trees). When I was still playing for the local cricket club, we had many a beer at the Lang Bome after the games. Sadly the old landmark eventually ceased to trade, and for a while it served as the headquarters of the De Mist commando.

Our town was mostly populated by blue-collar workers, employed at the SA Railways, or the large General Motors, Volkswagen or tyre factories in the Port Elizabeth and Uitenhage areas. Even though they had to commute some distance, people liked to live in Despatch, as there was more peace and quiet. We lived in Landman Street, which was just a plain dirt road like 90 per cent of the town's streets back then. Most of the houses in our area were modest dwellings built in the 1940s and 1950s. Today, many years later and after stints in Bloemfontein, Kimberley and Port Elizabeth, I live only a few blocks away from my boyhood home with my family – though now, thanks mainly to cricket, in a much larger and more modern house.

My father was a strict but fair man who believed in hard work. I'm not so sure he would have regarded full-time umpiring as a real job! As I said earlier, he spent a lot of time on the roads, and consequently I did not see as much of him as I would have liked. He passed away in 1987, at a time when I was standing in Bloemfontein in my inaugural first-class match. It was a game between Eastern Province and Free State, when Free State had a strong team with three international players in Alan Lamb, Sylvester Clarke and Alvin Kallicharran in their side.

My mother, Maria, was just as strict, and she did more than her share to keep food on the table. I remember her leaving before six in the morning to catch the train to Port Elizabeth, where she worked in a shoe factory, and returning only in the early evening. This meant that in my later high-school years, when my older sister was already out of the house and my younger sister was also working, I had to do some cooking in the afternoons so that there would be supper when my family got home. In between I had to do my schoolwork, a bit of gardening and tend to the chickens in the backyard, so there was little idle time for me then.

In my primary-school years, especially, my friends and I led a wonderful Huckleberry Finn–like childhood, which I wouldn't have traded for all the TV sets and PlayStations in the world. TV came to South Africa only in 1976, and in our time – thank goodness – we had to entertain ourselves, improvise and be creative.

A popular place for our adventures was the Swartkops River, originating in the Great Winterhoek Mountains and flowing past the town on the northern side on its way to the Indian Ocean. It was a favourite spot for fishing. We would catch carp, or *harders* (mullet), and in the evenings we would fish for freshwater eel in the eddies close to the river bank. The river was also the ideal place for swimming, or for paddling our crudely built canoes.

Beyond the river stretched a few miles of bush, which we explored thoroughly. Birdlife was abundant, and we learnt the name of every kind of bird. On the odd occasion one would see a rabbit, a small buck or even a jackal scurrying away into the undergrowth. Snakes also crossed our path, and we weren't scared of them – but we were careful, nevertheless.

At home we had some time to read comics, and once in a while we would go to the old Plaza bioscope in Uitenhage, where Westerns were our favourites. I recall one afternoon when the boys sat down all excitedly, waiting for a cowboy movie called *Oklahoma* to start. But we didn't realise that we were about to see a musical, and left in disgust when the cowboys started singing instead of shooting!

Like most of the kids who lived on the central and western sides of town, I attended the Susannah Fourie Primary School. Our big rival was the Sonop Primary School – in fact, the town's only other primary school at the time – on the eastern side. Few parents owned motor cars back then, so we foot-slogged to school and back every morning and afternoon, in the heat of summer and the chill of winter, dressed in our neat blue blazers and grey shorts. The English-speaking pupils – those who didn't attend Muir College and other schools in nearby Uitenhage – were accommodated in their own little school in the Dutch Reformed church hall. We didn't exactly fight the Boer War all over again, but there was a healthy rivalry between the Afrikaans and English lads.

Rugby had always been the big sport at both primary and high school, but we were also coached in cricket, tennis and athletics, and we competed mostly with schools from the Uitenhage, Port Elizabeth, Humansdorp and Sunday's River Valley areas. In primary school I played rugby for the Under-11s, and later for the Under-13s. Because I was a small lad, the coaches tried to hide me at fullback, but they did me no favours, as it was a nightmare trying to stop the bigger boys charging at me.

My favourite sport, though, was cricket. My first acquaintance with the game was at primary school. We only fielded a single Under-13 team, and games against other schools were few. But I just loved the sport and couldn't wait to get to the practices in the school nets in the afternoons. It was a passion that would determine the rest of my life.

Once in high school I played for the Under-14s, and by the age of 16 I made it into the first XI, but I probably had more enthusiasm than real talent. A few blocks away from where we lived there was an open park, but with hardly a small tree it was the ideal ground for our social rugby or cricket games. We had great fun playing cricket there, but the bad part was when we had to recover the ball from the yard of one of the houses across the park with the irate owner glaring at us through the window. Now our old playground and the adjacent old tennis clay courts are all gone, and in their place a retirement home was built many years ago.

Some of my fondest memories from those days revolve around the St George's Park Cricket Ground in Port Elizabeth, a venue where, years later, I would spend many an hour in the sun as club, provincial or Test umpire. Known as the Friendly City, Port Elizabeth was, of course, the home of the famous Pollock brothers, Peter and Graeme. Peter's cricketing talent was inherited by his son, Shaun, who captained South Africa before the current Proteas captain, Graeme Smith, took over.

On provincial match days we would take the train from Despatch to Port Elizabeth and then walk from the station all the way up the steep Donkin Hill to St George's Park. In the hour or two before the start of a match, we would go and watch guys like

Graeme Pollock or Eddie Barlow batting in the nets, preparing for the aggressive bowling assaults of a Mike Procter or Vince van der Bijl.

Graeme was simply unbelievable. He had the most wonderful timing and could hit a boundary with the greatest of ease. He never seemed to put much effort into his shots, but everyone knew that once he hit a ball, it stayed hit, as they say. *He* knew that too, and would nonchalantly lean back on his special heavy bat to watch the ball speeding towards the boundary. Graeme was never one for taking too many singles, for which he was often criticised. I'm sure he was just one of those extremely talented cricketers to whom a practice in the nets would not have made much difference. He was just a lad of 17, still in Grey High School, when he started making big scores for Eastern Province.

Years later, in 1987, I was acting as third umpire in the un-official Test in Port Elizabeth between South Africa and Kim Hughes's rebel Australian side when I found myself seated next to Graeme. It was to be his last unofficial Test. 'You can make a hundred today,' I said.

'If I do, I'll give you my shirt as a present,' he replied.

When his batting turn came, he walked onto the field with those characteristically long, easy strides, and went on to score 144 runs against a more than useful Australian side – at the age of 42. After his innings, one of the schoolboy attendants came to me with the message that 'Mr Pollock wants to see you in the changing room.' And there was Graeme, waiting to give me his shirt, just as he had promised. He also signed it for me, and today it is one of my most treasured possessions. There have been several memorabilia collectors who have made me some very good offers for it, but I've never been interested.

That match saw the curtain fall on the career of one of the world's finest batsmen of all time, and, incidentally, it also marked the debut for South Africa of a young Allan Donald, who wasn't going to become world famous as 'White Lightning' for nothing.

Peter Pollock's bowling was a joy to watch. He had a wonderfully fluent motion in his run-up, delivery action and follow-through, and it is hard to recall any top-class bowler of later years with as smooth an action as his.

How I loved the sounds and smells of cricket as a youngster! The leather ball against willow, the sharp thud as the ball hit the boundary pickets, the firm but polite clapping of the spectators. And the smells – linseed oil on bats, brand-new leather balls and freshly mowed outfields. Later, as an umpire out in the middle, I would continue to hear those sounds for another three decades. Over the years, though, the spectators' civilised applause had transformed into wild cheering and off-field antics – especially since the advent of the one-day version of the game.

The other main sport in most of our lives was rugby. A strong rugby culture existed in the Eastern Province then, and visiting provincial teams, even the mighty Blue Bulls, Western Province and Transvaal, always knew they were in for a rough time at Port Elizabeth's old Boet Erasmus Stadium. In those days there was still a clear break between summer and winter sport, so in summer it would be trips to St George's Park, in winter to the Boet Erasmus Stadium.

As South African kids, we grew up with the system of apartheid. We had no real comprehension of the situation; we were just kids who wanted to get on with our games. It never occurred to us that something was wrong here. The blacks all lived outside town, and the township for blacks – then called the *lokasie* (location) – lay beyond the hill and the town's graveyard, more or less out of sight from the town's whites. Those who had jobs were all involved in casual labour. Over the years the township has grown rapidly, and these days, two large townships, Daleview and Khayamandi, are bursting at the seams. Sadly, like in the rest of the country, work is hard to come by in the area, despite the existence of several industries.

It was only later in our young lives that we started to appreciate what it had all been about. On the sports front, at that stage, it did not affect our country significantly. It was only from 1970 onwards that we were deprived of watching any international cricket. That year, with really great players in their side like the Pollock brothers, Barry Richards, Eddie Barlow and Mike Procter, the Springboks annihilated Bill Lawry's Aussies in a five-Test series. But then the big blow fell: South Africa was banned from international cricket because of the government's policy of apartheid.

It was only in 1991, when Clive Rice's South African side visited India, that international competition was officially resumed. This event also gave me the opportunity to enter the Test scene as an umpire. In the meantime, our cricket fans had to be content with rebel teams from England, the West Indies and Australia – but more about that later.

I left my hometown in 1966 for Bloemfontein to do my apprenticeship as a carpenter with SA Railways, which I finished two years later. These skills have come in handy over the years, and at home I can brag with several pieces of furniture that I have crafted myself! In those days young men in South Africa were still conscripted for military training, and I ended up with the Infantry in Grahamstown, a historic Eastern Cape town that is also the home of Rhodes University.

The paratroopers division of the Defence Force had always held a certain fascination for me, so after my six months' basic training I applied for admission, passed my medical tests and went back to Bloemfontein for my paratrooper training in the Tempe area. At school I was a somewhat skinny lad, but after school I gained some weight, and by the time I'd finished my basic military training, I at least appeared to have enough flesh on my bones to survive the rigours of paratrooper training.

I don't know about today, but anyone who was in the army in those days will tell you that it was hard and demanding. I remember jogging in formation from our base with my fellow troopers, across the grassy Free State plains towards the low hills miles away in the distance. Often we would jog in small groups, carrying a thick pole on our shoulders, with some hard-arse corporal or sergeant jogging alongside, while we sang to the beat of our footfall. Sometimes the guys made up their own lyrics, and some of those songs you wouldn't sing in front of your mother. It was a tough period, but to use that old cliché, I believe it helped build character.

Of course the parachuting part of our training was something special. To get the hang of jumping with a parachute, we first jumped from a high platform – nicknamed the *aapkas* (monkey box) – aided by pulleys and so on, until the big day arrived when we jumped from the old Dakota, and later the T130-Hercules aeroplane from a few thousand feet up in the sky. What a sensation that was! The rush of wind as you hurled yourself away from the door of the plane, the sudden jerk through your body as the parachute opened, the amazing perspective of the landscape below, closing in as you descend. To make life even more interesting, we would have jumps in the dark of night, or into dams. Somehow I survived it all, and I was awarded my 'wings' as proof.

One had the option of signing on for an extra year after completion of a year's military training, which I decided to do. Those were the early years of the South African Border War, and I spent a lot of time working in the construction of border bases in Katima Mulilo and elsewhere. For those who don't know the area, Katima Mulilo lies directly on the banks of the Zambezi River and at the eastern tip of the Caprivi Strip of Namibia (then known as South West Africa). I worked in the Caprivi bases until 1971, when I returned to civilian life.

I moved back to Despatch to ply my trade as a carpenter in the Railways, where I would stay until 1975. During those five years I played cricket for the town's first XI, which took part in the Eastern Province 2A league. I was never a good batsman – or anything special as a bowler, until I played club cricket in

Kimberley – but I was a good fielder. My proudest moment in those days was when I won the Union Cricket Club fielding trophy for junior club players one year. My enthusiasm was further rewarded in 1974, when the club appointed me as secretary. It was my first exposure to the administration of the game.

That was also when I first became aware of Ian Howell, who would later become an international umpire, when he and his twin brother, David, played for Grey High School against the club as 15-year-olds. Boy, were these two lads full of cricket! Their father, Eddie, was a household name in Eastern Province umpiring circles, having been the secretary of the South African Umpires Association between 1962 and 1969. Ian later played more than a hundred games for Eastern Province and Border, while David played for Eastern Province, Transvaal and Border.

After he retired as a player, Ian turned to umpiring, and it was a matter of weeks before he handled his first provincial match. Not everyone was happy with his rapid promotion, but I think the fact that he had been a provincial player helped a lot. Ian made his Test debut in early 2001 in the second Test between South Africa and Sri Lanka at Newlands, and today he is one of the more experienced umpires on the international circuit.

Our club celebrated its 50th anniversary in December 1999. It was a memorable occasion for both the club and the town, and the guest speaker was none other than Proteas captain Hansie Cronjé. Little did we know at the time that he was heavily involved in fixing match results at international level and that, less than a year later, he would be the focus of an official investigation into match fixing. But more about that, and the Hansie I knew, later.

In 1975 I was admitted to the works supervisor exams of the Railways, and once I had passed the exams, I got a job in Kimberley as the youngest foreman on the Railways at that stage. It was here, in the City of Diamonds, that I turned to umpiring.

It was a move that would change my world forever.

2

From the Railways to the cricket pitch

" *Obviously I was as pleased as punch to stand in my first provincial match, but after the game Hylton Ackerman slated the three lbw decisions I had given during the match – even though two had gone against Griquas and only one against Western Province. 'You don't have a bloody clue what an lbw is,' Hylton snarled at me.* **"**

When I arrived in Kimberley, I had a choice to join either the Hoffe Park Railways Club or the De Beers Club. I was advised to try the latter, and so I stepped into one of the oldest clubs in the country. The Griqualand West Cricket Union boasts a long and colourful history, and celebrated its centenary in 1991, when they hosted a game between Griquas and Free State. Interestingly, Hansie Cronjé and future Proteas coach Mickey Arthur featured in the Free State line-up. Some of the older folk in town could even recall the historic visit of the Marylebone Cricket Club (MCC) in 1938 when they played Griqualand West at the Athletic Club Ground, and England legends like Len Hutton (who scored 149) and Wally Hammond graced the field.

I found the De Beers Club, where the former England wicket-keeper Dave Bairstow was reigning as coach, an organised set-up.

I learnt a lot from Bairstow while I was there. Although I developed more as a player, I have to admit that I was never much of a batsman, while my bowling action was suspect. Ironically, I was dropped from the De Beers side after claiming 10 wickets in a match, which led to a bit of a quarrel between me and the selectors. The upshot was that I decided to call it a day as a player and try my hand at umpiring. Never could I have guessed on what a long and rewarding road this decision would take me.

At the time, Don Lee was the chairman of the Griqualand West Referees Society. Determined to wear the white coat, I approached Don, who entered me for an umpire's exam. My enthusiasm was rewarded when I scored 94 per cent. I was ready for my first match, happy to stand in any match of any league. But Don had nothing for me for the first weekend after the exam. Then later he told me that I could umpire in a club game between Pirates and De Beers (my old club!) along with Roger Symcox, the father of future Proteas spinner Pat Symcox. The Symcox family had been synonymous with Griqualand West cricket for many years, and Pat had a good innings with Griquas before he sought greener pastures in Northern Transvaal and Natal to eventually become a Test player. At that stage Roger was already serving on the Currie Cup panel, and I was looking forward to partnering such an experienced umpire in my first match.

On the Saturday before the match I was both excited and nervous. I consoled myself with the thought that good old Roger, with all his experience, would be there to gently guide me through the turbulence of my first club match as umpire. But he wasn't. When I arrived at the field, I heard that Roger had gone to play bowls – his other great love in life. At such short notice no other umpire could be found, so, in the end, after a chat with the two captains, it was decided that I would stand as the only umpire. And so it happened that in my very first game I never stood at square leg, but was staring down the pitch from either end throughout the whole match!

As keen as mustard, I called 17 no-balls and wides. And lo and behold, my old club De Beers lost – their first defeat in eight seasons! You can bet that quite a few snide remarks were made in my direction. Maybe they were thinking I was taking some sort of revenge ... I don't know. But I stood my ground and told them, 'If you want to play the game the way you want to, I will walk off and you can do the job yourselves.'

I stood in my first provincial game much sooner than I'd hoped or was officially supposed to. According to the rules at the time, an umpire had to have officiated in at least 21 first-league club matches before he could be considered for provincial duty. But Don Lee bent the rules, and after only eight first-league games he gave me a chance to umpire in a match between Griqualand West and Western Province B in Kimberley, in December 1981. Province had a good side, featuring players like their captain, the well-known Hylton Ackerman, future South African spinner Omar Henry and Bossie Clarke.

Obviously I was as pleased as punch to stand in my first provincial match, but after the game Hylton Ackerman slated the three lbw decisions I had given during the match – even though two had gone against Griquas and only one against Western Province.

'You don't have a bloody clue what an lbw is,' Hylton snarled at me.

Ironically, when the same sides met again two weeks later in Cape Town, the two umpires dished out no fewer than 14 lbw decisions, seven against each side. And when Griquas captain Mike Doherty met me in Kimberley soon afterwards, he said, 'I have a message for you from Hylton Ackerman. He says he wished there had been 10 of your kind at the match in Cape Town!' I felt much better about the whole thing then. One weekend an experienced and respected guy like Hylton flayed me, only for me to receive unexpected praise from him two weekends later!

Apart from the fact that that game was my first provincial outing, I remember it for another significant reason. My father never really supported me in my career, but that day he was sitting in the pavilion, and at some stage he whistled and waved at me. Granted, he was visiting my sister Marie, who also lived in Kimberley at the time, but at least he had come to watch me in my first game at provincial level. However, it was the only game in which I umpired that he ever bothered to attend.

As for my mother, she wasn't interested in sport at all. In my later years, as international umpire, she would once in a while turn on the TV to see where in the world I was umpiring, but the game itself was of little, if any, interest to her.

I returned to Port Elizabeth in 1982, working as a technical superintendent in the Railways building industry. The following year I joined the Eastern Province Umpires Association. I found it difficult to gain a spot on the provincial panel, as experienced guys like Sandy Matthews, Barry Lambson and Falie Payne were still active. By that stage I had to juggle my time between my job and umpiring, to the extent that my bosses finally gave me an ultimatum: either you stop umpiring, or you accept a package from us and leave. I chose the latter.

I then landed a job as a building inspector with the Department of Education, which, like my previous job, demanded a lot of my time. After six years I faced the same dilemma as in the Railways, and that was when, in 2000, I became a full-time umpire.

I'd hoped that my provincial umpiring career would continue after I left the Railways, but it was only in 1987, four years after joining the Eastern Province Umpires Association, that I was awarded a provincial match. I was appointed to stand in my first Bowl match in Grahamstown in a game between Eastern Province and Natal with Brian Basson, who later became the chairman of the United Cricket Board of South Africa.

During those early years, I suffered one of the greatest embarrassments of my career. I was standing with fellow umpire Peter

Wildman in a match between Eastern Province B and Western Province B on the old Union Club field in Port Elizabeth, and at some stage a left-handed and a right-handed batsman joined each other at the crease. After a while I got too lazy to walk over to square leg once the batsmen had crossed for a run, and I simply remained standing in the same spot – so sometimes I would be standing square towards the batsman on the on-side, then again square towards the off-side.

I don't know where my thoughts were wandering, but at some point I realised that there were four fielders behind square instead of only two, as the laws prescribed. Instinctively I called a no-ball from where I stood, which caused quite a bit of consternation among the players.

'What was that for?' the fielding captain asked.

'You have more than two players behind square leg,' I answered. 'In fact, I'm counting four.'

At that moment I was standing square to the off-side of the batting crease and not on the leg side, where I should have been. So of course I'd been counting the two slip fielders as well – which, of course, the players gleefully pointed out to me. Realising my mistake, I feebly apologised and stood there with a sheepish grin on my face, but believe me, at the time there wasn't a hole in the ground big enough to swallow me! And from then on I made sure that I switched positions when the batsmen crossed.

I had a memorable first match in the A-section of the Castle Currie Cup. It was played in 1987 in Bloemfontein, between Eastern Province and the newcomers to the A-section, the Free State.

At the time, Dr Ali Bacher, CEO of South African Cricket, was keen to promote the Free State to the A-section, and as a result they were allowed to contract three professional players from overseas. These happened to be quite formidable cricketers: West Indians Sylvester Clarke and Alvin Kallicharran, and England batsman Allan Lamb, who had moved to England from South Africa some years previously. A blossoming Allan Donald also featured in the side, while at the same time Mike Procter, having just retired as a player, was appointed as the first full-time coach for Free State. The results were spectacular, and at the end of the competition, Free State faced Transvaal's 'Mean Machine', with the uncompromising Clive Rice at the helm, in the final. Unfortunately for Free State, they were devastated on a typical 'green mamba' at the Wanderers.

In their match against Eastern Province, in which I umpired, the Free Staters were still on their way to the final, with Allan Lamb in brilliant form, setting new records along the way. In this particular match he scored a splendid 274 runs – a new South African provincial record. But I also remember the encounter well for the hard time Kallicharran gave me questioning my decisions and, secondly, for Sylvester Clarke's match-winning six off former Australian Rod McCurdy's final ball.

It is interesting to note that when Lamb had to go back to England, it paved the way for a young rising star named Hansie Cronjé to make his debut for Free State in the final. Little did I know that this fresh-faced youngster would go on to captain South Africa and that our paths would cross many times in the future.

Kallicharran was a difficult customer, and his actions drove Lou Rautenbach to cheat for the only time in his 40-year umpiring career. The incident occurred in a Transvaal/Free State match in Bloemfontein, in which Lou stood with me.

At one stage, Kallicharran was batting and he got a nick. I gave him out. When he walked past Lou at square leg, he said some unrepeatable things about me. Lou was very upset about it. He went up to Joubert Strydom, who was the Free State captain, and said: 'This man swore at my colleague, so I'm going to report him.' Kallicharran was subsequently fined R500, which was a fair amount of money in those days.

Then, the very next weekend, Lou and I stood together again in a Benson & Hedges game between Free State and Natal in Durban. We were inspecting the ground when Lou said to me,

'Do you see what I see? There's no TV here tonight. That guy from Free State, you leave him to me. I'll sort him out.' I wasn't sure what 'sorting out' Lou had in mind, but I soon discovered.

At some point Kallicharran was batting, with Hansie Cronjé at the non-striker's end. Kallicharran played forward to a ball but didn't play a shot, and the ball hit him high on the pads. To his horror, Lou gave him out. Kallicharran stood his ground, but Lou told him in no uncertain terms, 'Mr Kallicharran, you are out, my friend. If you don't walk, there's another 500 bucks for you.'

Standing next to Lou, Hansie sarcastically asked him, 'Do you feel better now, Oom Lou?'

'Yes,' Lou said with a straight face, 'but the problem is Rudi also wanted to stick him!'

At the age of 72, Lou was still umpiring in club games in 2009. He farms with cattle in the Zuurberg, about 130 kilometres outside Port Elizabeth, but he loves the game as much as I do and will travel 260 kilometres on a Saturday, and more often than not on the Sunday as well, for umpiring duties. Incidentally, Lou has the distinction, along with Ossie Schooff, of becoming the first umpire in the history of the game to stand in two ODIs on the same day. In 1986 at Newlands, South Africa hammered a rebel Australian side in no time at all, and the teams decided to play another game for the packed-out crowd.

One of my biggest disappointments of this period was being overlooked as umpire for the Benson & Hedges final between Western Province and Natal. Robbie Brooks and Karl Liebenberg got the nod ahead of me, and I was appointed as third umpire. It was some consolation when the two captains, Adrian Kuiper and Peter Rawson, handed me their shirts after the match. Brian Basson, who became chief of South African umpires, used to re-assure me, 'Just hang in there. Your chance will come.' After a long time waiting I would merely reply, 'My arms are getting paralysed from all the waiting.'

But a year later I was again ignored, this time not even

making the final three. Only a hole-in-one on the seventh hole at Uitenhage's golf course helped to improve my mood!

Speaking of golf ... That game caused me great embarrassment once, when I was handling a match between Western Province and Transvaal in the mid-1990s. The match had become dour and boring, and I was standing at square leg. It seemed the perfect time to practise my shadow golf shots. The players were keeping an eye on me from the pitch, and I was just at the end of my follow-through when suddenly there was a loud appeal. Looking up, I saw the stumps shattered and the batsman, Western Province's Daryll Cullinan, out of his crease.

'Not out,' I said quickly.

'Why not?' asked the Transvaal wicketkeeper, Nic Pothas.

'I didn't see it,' I replied.

It transpired that while I wasn't looking, Pothas had pushed Cullinan out of his crease and knocked over the stumps, appealing for a stumping at the same time. The players were taking the mickey out of me.

We all had a good laugh and the game went on.

The 1980s were a frustrating time for me, as they were for most South Africans, watching our cricket union trying to please local fans by staging rebel tours from various countries. Nineteen eighty-two to 1990 was a sad era for our top cricketers. Many of them could have become international legends had they been given the chance on the official international stage. One can only imagine what the likes of Graeme Pollock, Barry Richards, Mike Procter, Clive Rice, Peter Kirsten, Vince van der Bijl or Garth le Roux might have achieved with bat or ball.

I was a youngster in 1966/67 when Bob Simpson led his Australian team to South Africa for a five-Test series, which the Springboks, as they were still called in those days, won 3-1, with one Test drawn. The great Graeme Pollock scored a total of 537 runs at an average of 76.71, which included one innings of 209 runs.

South Africa were due to play England at home in 1968/69, but tensions stemming from the John Vorster government's apartheid policy came to a head when South African–born Basil D'Oliveira, who was of Cape coloured ancestry, was chosen for England to replace the injured Tom Cartwright. Vorster's view was that it had become 'the team of the anti-apartheid movement', and he refused to allow them to enter South Africa with D'Oliveira in the team. Consequently, the tour was cancelled.

But we did get a last Test series before our expulsion from international cricket when Bill Lawry's Australians toured here in 1970. Coming off a gruelling tour of India, they were routed by the Springboks. Pollock, again, was in tremendous form when he broke Jackie McGlew's South African Test record of 255, scoring 274 in the second Test in Durban. His record stood for nearly 30 years, until Daryll Cullinan scored 275 not out against New Zealand in 1999. It is a great pity that Graeme Pollock's Test career was brought to an end through isolation when he was only 26 years of age.

The top players felt the international isolation keenly, and they looked at measures to try to reverse the looming sporting boycott. I remember the huge stir it caused when, during a match in 1971 to celebrate the 10th anniversary of the formation of the Republic of South Africa, the players from both teams walked off after one ball, issuing a joint statement that read: 'We cricketers feel that the time has come for an expression of our views. We fully support the South African Cricket Association's application to invite non-whites to tour Australia, if they are good enough, and further subscribe to merit being the only criterion on the cricket field.'

The large conservative element in the country was horrified by their action, labelling them 'liberalists' and 'communists', and the government refused to budge; from then on we had to make do with all kinds of rebel tours.

When Graham Gooch's rebel side from England arrived in

South Africa in March 1982, only Pollock, Richards and Procter had had official Test experience – dating back as far as 1970, when the Springboks had demolished the Aussies in the four-Test series. The touring side did include top players like Geoff Boycott, Alan Knott, Dennis Amiss, Derek Underwood and Chris Old – and, of course, Bob Woolmer – but we all knew it wasn't the real thing. So it was difficult to get excited about the South Africans' 1-0 'series' win against the English.

The same applied when the Arosa Sri Lanka side toured the same year, the West Indies toured in 1982/83 and 1983/84, the Australians in 1985/86 and 1986/87 (a side that included South African–born Kepler Wessels), and England in 1990.

I got my first taste of 'international' cricket umpiring in 1990, when Mike Gatting's rebel side from England toured South Africa on the first of two proposed tours. The first tour kicked off in late January, and about two weeks prior to the start, the South African Cricket Board appointed a panel of eight umpires from which six were to be chosen to officiate in the first three three-day matches of the tour. I was very pleased to be one of them. Others on the panel who became international umpires later were Karl Liebenberg, Cyril Mitchley and Barry Lambson.

I could recall how our umpires had been heavily criticised during Kim Hughes's first Australian rebel tour in 1985/86, and in fact some of them retired because of it. The idea was now for the top umpires and the players to get used to one another before the start of the 'Test' series.

I got my chance to stand when the touring side played the South African Universities in Bloemfontein. John Emburey captained the visitors, while Hansie Cronjé and his brother Frans (12th man) featured in the students' line-up. Some of the players in the students' team, like Andrew Hudson, Clive Eksteen, Tertius Bosch and Rudolf Steyn, later represented South Africa. My mentor and good friend from Griqualand West, Roger Symcox, partnered me in the match. This time he didn't go and play bowls!

Unfortunately the tour – perhaps fortunately, in retrospect – caused great racial tension in the country, coinciding as it did with the unbanning of the ANC and the release of Nelson Mandela. At the time, Ali Bacher stressed that the tour was divisive, and of course the South African Cricket Board, under great political pressure, cancelled the second Gatting tour. Ironically, this paved the way for the creation of the United Cricket Board of South Africa (UCBSA) in June the following year and, subsequently, South Africa's readmission to international cricket.

I was due to stand in the one 'Test' in Durban, but the cancellation of the tour brought a quick end to my 'Test' aspirations. Fortunately my chance came two years later, when India became the first side to officially tour South Africa after readmission.

The future looked good for South African cricket, with plenty of international cricket to come, and there was a lot to look forward to from an umpiring point of view. South Africa was invited to the 1992 Cricket World Cup, but prior to the tournament, in November 1991, an official South African side, led by a 42-year-old Clive Rice – who was still as competitive as ever – left for India for three ODIs. Thus he became South Africa's first captain after readmission.

At the time, I thought he was the right man for the job. A no-nonsense skipper, Clive had always set high standards for himself and his players and he was the man for the big occasion. Ali Bacher went along as manager, with Mike Procter as coach. For the record, India won the first two matches and South Africa the third.

The South Africans' first experience of cricket in India was unforgettable. In their first match, at Eden Gardens, some 100 000 spectators packed the stadium, and from beginning to end the noise was deafening. People shouted and screamed and fireworks went off … In this intimidating atmosphere, the Proteas never really stood a chance. In subsequent years I would experience those same conditions. Imagine having to pick up a nick by a batsman in that cacophony of deafening noise!

The Indian side was led by Mohammad Azharuddin, who was later exposed and banned for match fixing. And in the South African side was a young development player named Hansie Cronjé, who would also go on trial and be banned for the same transgression – but more on that later. Also in the Indian team was 18-year-old Sachin Tendulkar, who had made his Test debut as a 16-year-old in 1989. Already, he was a class player: 11 Tests, one century to his name and an average of close to 40. Our paths would cross the next year, in my very first Test, under not-so-pleasant circumstances.

3

The international stage

❝ *In an interview with a British radio station I replied that I would be happy to look at video replays and apologise if I had made mistakes. 'I would be lying if I say that I never make mistakes,' I said, 'but I am an honest umpire.'* **❞**

When South Africa was readmitted to international cricket, the UCBSA appointed me as one of six umpires who would operate on the basis of a rotation system in Tests. India was due to tour South Africa in December 1992, and I was pleased as pie when I was awarded the Test at St George's Park in Port Elizabeth, my home ground. I was to do duty on the field for the first three days and spend the last two days behind the TV monitor. It was a historic Test in the sense that it was to be the first series to see the use of TV replays to assist in umpiring decisions.

Two weeks before the Test, I had a chance to have a look at the players in my very first ODI, also in the Friendly City. My fellow umpire in the match was Cyril Mitchley. Not a memorable match from a spectator's point of view, though, as India was dismissed for 147 in the 50th over, and Kepler Wessels's men passed that score with six wickets intact and a few overs remaining.

The game did, however, produce some unpleasantness when Kapil Dev ran out Peter Kirsten, the non-striker, when he backed up too far before the ball was delivered. It has to be said that Kapil Dev had warned Kirsten at least twice in earlier matches that this could happen. We, the umpires, had to give Kirsten out. Kepler thought Dev's appeal unsporting and he got into an argument with the fielders, and on top of it Kirsten refused to go until he was signalled to leave the field. He was later fined for dissent.

The Test was only two weeks away, and for most of that time I had butterflies fluttering around in my stomach. This was going to be an international Test – the real thing. It helped a lot when, prior to the Test, I had a good chat with Kepler Wessels. An experienced former Australian Test cricketer, he was familiar with the hard world of international cricket, and he is a man with a great work ethic and immense self-discipline.

'Rudi, because it's your first Test, [the players] are going to take their chances with you,' he warned. 'That I can assure you. Don't allow them to put pressure on you.' It was sound advice.

In the early 1990s, especially just after South Africa's readmission to international cricket, players did put additional pressure on South African umpires. It was as if they thought they could take more chances with us because we were South Africans – as if the country now owed the world something! This belief was added to the perception that our umpires were 'rusty', because of 22 years of international isolation. I know that South Africa's top rugby referees – André Watson, for example – had similar experiences in those early days after South Africa's readmission to international sport.

I have since learnt that the more severe the pressure, the more thick-skinned you have to be. This attitude has helped me survive in the jungle that is international cricket umpiring. And it *is* a jungle out there, believe me. I recall South African umpire Barry Lambson being in tears after a match between South Africa and New Zealand at Newlands when the pressure and criticism finally got to him. Umpires are mere human beings, after all.

Finally the day of the Test arrived. On 26 December 1992, I walked out onto the St George's Park pitch with Dave Shepherd to stand in the first of my more than 100 Tests. But of course I never dreamt of going that far at the time. Wilf Diedricks sat upstairs as third umpire. I also stood on-field with Dave the next day, with Wilf on day three, and upstairs as TV umpire on days four and five.

By Test standards it was a fairly low-scoring affair, but it was a good start for the home boys on their return to the Test arena, anyway. India only managed to get 212 in their first innings, with Allan Donald living up to his nickname of White Lightning, taking 5/55. In reply, South Africa recovered from a shaky start – Kepler Wessels bowled for a duck by Manoj Prabhakar – when Hansie Cronjé stabilised their innings with a gritty 135 before he was bowled by Anil Kumble.

In their second innings, despite a knock of 129 by the great Kapil Dev, India was restricted to only 215. And again lightning struck in the form of Donald, with figures of 7/84. That left South Africa with 155 runs to win, which they reached with only one wicket down. Typically, Kepler, the South African captain, compensated for his first-innings lapse with 95 not out.

But probably my most vivid recollection of the match was the dismissal of Tendulkar. The fiery South African fast bowler Brett Schultz was having a go at the Indian batsmen from my side of the pitch when Tendulkar nicked one to wicketkeeper Dave Richardson. The South African fielders appealed loudly, and I gave Tendulkar the slow death sign. As he walked back to the pavilion he had tears in his eyes, and he told me that he wasn't out. Putting on an act? Although there were TV replays in those days, there were no Snickometers, so we'll never know for certain.

I have had the privilege of watching Sachin bat for many years after that game. What a wonderful player he is. A small man, but big in heart and match temperament. And arguably the finest player of spin bowling I have seen in my time.

It took a few years before I stood in my next Test – until 2 January 1997, in fact. It was also the year that I became a full-time ICC umpire. In those years, the custom was to use local umpires for Test cricket; in South Africa we had six umpires, and they all had to be given a chance out in the middle. In addition, much less Test cricket was played then than in the present.

The Test, again, involved South Africa and India, but this time the venue was the picturesque Newlands in Cape Town. I recall the match for producing runs galore. In South Africa's first innings of 529/7, Gary Kirsten, Brian McMillan and Lance Klusener (at no. 9) all scored centuries. India replied with 359, with Tendulkar in fine form with 169 and Azharuddin also scoring a hundred. Declaring on 256/6 in their second innings, the Proteas left India with a big score to win the match, and indeed it was well beyond them. They succumbed for a mere 144 runs.

I stood in two more Tests in 1997. One was when the Proteas played Australia in Port Elizabeth, and the other featured my first overseas appearance, in Colombo, where Sri Lanka hosted India.

When Australia toured South Africa three years earlier, I had my first opportunity to become better acquainted with the big Australian names in international cricket. I didn't handle a Test, but I did stand with Cyril Mitchley in the Aussies' match against the President's XI in Potchefstroom. What a strong Aussie side that was! Captained by Allan Border, it included the Waugh brothers, Mark Taylor, David Boon, Big Merv Hughes and then, of course, great stars of the future like Shane Warne, Matthew Hayden and Glenn McGrath.

When the Aussies toured South Africa again in 1997, Mark Taylor skippered the side, and by then Hayden, Warne and McGrath were well-established players – *and* they still had Steve and Mark Waugh to count on. As mentioned, I was appointed to stand in the second Test at St George's Park in Port Elizabeth; my partner was Srini Venkataraghavan from India, with South Africa's Dave Orchard acting as TV umpire.

It was a memorable match. The South Africans, skippered by Hansie Cronjé, only managed 209 runs in their first innings. Warne bowled well, taking 3/62, but Jason Gillespie was even better with 5/45. Australia must have fancied their chances of an early victory, but a big shock awaited them. Their 108 runs in their first innings turned out to be their second-lowest Test total ever against South Africa. One couldn't believe that such a talented side could slump so dramatically, but that's cricket for you. And when South Africa's first wicket in their second innings fell only at 87, everyone thought that there could be only one winner – Hansie's boys. But then South Africa lost their remaining nine wickets for only 81 runs and it was left to a brilliant Mark Waugh with 116 to steer Australia to a nail-biting two-wicket victory and a 2-0 lead in the series.

The Test at the Sinhalese Sports Club (SSC) Ground in Colombo was the second of a two-match series, and while the Test was drawn (as was the first), I saw a lot of runs being scored and had the privilege of watching the great Sri Lankan names like Jayasuriya, Jayawardene and Muralitharan in action. I recall centuries from Rahul Dravid and Sourav Ganguly, a fine four-wicket spell from Muralitharan, and finally Jayasuriya being bowled with his score on 199. Jayasuriya rewrote the record books with 571 runs in the two-match series, which beat the previous record of Wally Hammond for England against New Zealand in 1932/33. So for me it was time well spent in Colombo.

When Hansie Cronjé's Proteas took on Pakistan in the third Test of their three-match series in March 1998, it was also my third Test at St George's Park in Port Elizabeth. South Africa faced the formidable pace duo of Waqar Younis – who picked up 6/78 in the first innings – and Shoaib Akhtar. I can't remember an opening pair quicker than these two. That's tremendous pressure from both sides for any batsman. Allan Donald wasn't bad himself, taking 4/47 and 4/27 in Pakistan's two innings. But, for me, the game marked the potential of the 21-year-old Mark Boucher, whose 10 dismissals equalled Dave Richardson's record for the St George's ground. (Eleven years later, in the 2009/10 season, Boucher was still a stalwart in the Proteas side, sharing Man of the Series with Graeme Swann of England at the end of the South Africa/England Test series.) Winning by 259 runs at St George's, the Proteas managed a one-all series draw.

Hardly three weeks later, I officiated at Centurion, standing in the second Test between South Africa and Sri Lanka, where I could watch some great spin bowling by Muralitharan. He bowled Gary Kirsten with one of the best balls I've seen in my career, and he recorded a five-wicket haul for the 12th time in Test cricket. But then Hansie Cronjé exploded the myth that South African batsmen cannot play spin. He destroyed Muralitharan's 17th over by hitting a four and three consecutive sixes, all over mid-wicket, scoring 50 off just 31 balls. His innings eventually led his side to a six-wicket victory and set up a 2-0 series triumph against the tourists.

I officiated in three more Tests over the rest of the year, paying a second visit to Colombo, where I stood in the first Test between New Zealand and Sri Lanka. Predictably, in oppressive heat in Colombo, it was the spinners who had the most impact. The Kiwi spinners Paul Wiseman and Daniel Vettori shared eight wickets to bowl New Zealand to a 167-run victory over Sri Lanka. Needing 465 to win, Sri Lanka collapsed from 194/2 at lunch to 297 all out.

I also made my first visit to Harare that October, where Zimbabwe took on India, and I stood in my hometown in the Proteas' game against the West Indies – my first acquaintance with the boys from the Caribbean. Of these three series, the one in Harare was, surprisingly, the most remarkable. It was David against Goliath, and I had the privilege to watch one of the biggest upsets of the decade. Scoring 221 in their first innings to India's 280, Zimbabwe followed up with 293 in their second outing, leaving the strong Indian batting line-up with only 235 to win. But Zimbabwe bowled them out for 173 to record their finest cricketing hour.

I enjoyed it as a great Test match in which fortunes fluctuated dramatically from one day to the next. Until that game, Zimbabwe had only won a Test match once, on the same Harare Sports Club ground, in 1995 against Pakistan. Not even the absence through injury of two of their top players, Grant Flower and Guy Whittall, stood in their way. One could sense the determination of the Zimbabweans as they went out after lunch, and once they'd gained the upper hand, they never let go.

The West Indies toured South Africa for a five-Test series in the 1998/99 season, their first official visit to the country. Previous contests had consisted of rebel tours during the sports isolation years, as mentioned earlier. I was appointed to stand in the second (St George's Park) and fifth (Centurion) Tests of the series. Having won the first Test, the Proteas scored a crushing 178-run victory over the West Indies at St George's Park. The West Indies had to make 320 to win on a lively pitch and they were simply never in contention. South Africa went on to win the third and fourth Tests as well, and in the final Test in January 1999, at Centurion, in which I officiated as on-field umpire, they completed a 5-0 series whitewash, crushing the West Indies by 351 runs with a day to spare.

It was a one-sided series, but at least I saw the fastest century in South African Test-cricket history being recorded in South Africa's second innings by one of my favourite players, Jonty Rhodes, who scored a sensational 103 not out off only 95 balls. The previous record was held by teammate Lance Klusener, set two seasons before against India at Newlands off 102 balls. During Jonty's innings there was some doubt about whether a boundary he'd hit had been a four or a six, but we signalled a six. As he approached his hundred, there was therefore some confusion as to whether he needed an extra two runs for his century. The changing room sent Jonty a message that he should get the two runs to make sure he got his hundred. But I told him to relax – we had already made the decision about the boundary in question and it had indeed been a six.

It was a humiliating series for the West Indies, who, for the first time in their history, lost all their matches in a five-Test series. The victory enabled South Africa to complete their most successful series ever, the previous best being when they beat Australia 4-0 in a four-match series in 1969/70 – the last Test matches before the country was isolated from world cricket for 21 years. Proteas all-rounder Jacques Kallis was named Man of the Series, having scored 485 runs at an average of just under 70 and taking 17 wickets.

Travelling far and wide had become part and parcel of my life as an umpire, and in between these Tests I made a quick visit to Hamilton in New Zealand, where the Kiwis took on India in the third Test of their series. The match was drawn, but Rahul Dravid entertained the crowd, and me, with two consecutive centuries (190 and 103 not out), as did the hard-hitting Chris Cairns with 126.

I had my first exposure to the heavy demands of umpiring on the Indian subcontinent soon after, when I stood in the second Sri Lanka/India match in the Asian Test Championship at the SSC in Colombo. Rajesh Ramesh, Dravid and Tendulkar scored hundreds for India, but Mahela Jayawardene stole the show with a big 242 for Sri Lanka. But rain had the final say, and we later had to call off play. I also handled the third match of the championship – another drawn match – between Pakistan and Sri Lanka in the Gaddafi Stadium in Lahore. Ten years later the stadium would hit the news after a terrifying terrorist attack on the visiting Sri Lankan cricket team. And then some people think cricket is a safe way of life … Despite the draw, Pakistan's Wajahatullah Wasti provided the highlight with two consecutive centuries.

Then, on 22 July 1999 came the moment I had been dreaming of as an umpire for years – standing in a Test at Lord's, the traditional home of cricket. I had had the honour of tasting the Lord's ground experience when I'd officiated in the opening match of the 1999 World Cup held in England in May, but that, of course, had been a one-day affair.

Once you have entered the ground through the pair of orna-mental WG Grace Memorial Gates at the St John's Wood Road entrance, you know you're in a special place with a unique atmos-phere. So what a moment it was when I walked out onto the field with the England and New Zealand players for the second Test of their four-match series.

But I didn't bring the English any luck. England scored 186 in their first innings, to which the Kiwis replied with 358. England's second innings wasn't much better, and they could scrape together only 229. Left a target of 58 runs, a New Zealand victory was never in doubt, and they eventually won by nine wickets. It was only New Zealand's fifth win in 80 Tests against England, their first win at Lord's in 13 attempts, and their first win in England since 1986. So after the match the beer flowed in the New Zealand dressing room.

Later that year, in October, I had my first outing as umpire in India, the land of Sunil Gavaskar, Kapil Dev and Sachin Tendulkar. The Test, the third between the home side and New Zealand, was played in the Sardar Patel Stadium, Ahmedabad. And Tendulkar made my visit well worth it with a superb double century in India's first innings of 583, to which Ganguly and Ramesh also added centuries. Facing 494 balls, Tendulkar gave me plenty of time to watch a maestro in action. The match was eventually drawn, but India took the series 1-0.

Back home in December, I stood in my hometown again, when England took on the Proteas at St George's Park in the second Test of their Millennium Series. But it doesn't hold too pleasant memories.

The match was drawn, with Lance Klusener and Michael Atherton scoring hundreds each. But it needed a Jacques Kallis half-century to steer South Africa to a possible victory on the last day. South Africa had stood on a shaky 48/2 when Kallis, on 12, pushed at a ball, which, it later showed, was actually caught by Chris Adams. But I didn't give Kallis out, and as a result I wasn't the most popular man with the England players. They didn't even applaud Kallis's subsequent half-century. During the catch incident, Dave Orchard, as TV umpire, looked at replays from the SABC and was unable to find conclusive evidence that the ball had carried. So he gave the green light to Kallis, but Sky Television's pictures revealed a fair catch. It goes to show what a difference a camera angle can make.

In pursuit of their second-innings target, England captain Nasser Hussain defied all South African attempts to dislodge him, and when the game was called off with two overs remaining, England had four wickets standing. But they were very unhappy with some of the decisions, like Alec Stewart being ruled lbw by Steve Bucknor, and Chris Adams, whom I had given out as caught off a bat–pad. They were also unhappy that I had not given Boucher out in the first innings and Kirsten in the second, and for slow-deathing Mark Butcher and Michael Vaughan in the second innings.

After the match Steve Bucknor and I were heavily criticised in the British press for what they labelled 'dubious' decisions. Former England players Ian Botham and Geoff Boycott also added their pennies' worth, Botham pleading that the ICC should do away with local umpires in Test matches. He said that it no longer made sense to have just one neutral umpire in a Test. Why do things by half measures? Why not do it right? he asked. He added that he was not suggesting I was a cheat, but asked how I could have been appointed to stand in my hometown, where I'd be under tremendous pressure.

In an interview with a British radio station I replied that I would be happy to look at video replays and apologise if I had made mistakes. 'I would be lying if I say that I never make mistakes,' I said, 'but I am an honest umpire.' I also couldn't see the need for two overseas umpires, as all umpires are supposed to be honest – whether you are standing at home or away.

An unusual bowling incident had also occurred, when Lance Klusener delivered a ball to Nasser Hussain from 15 metres behind the stumps, and Steve Bucknor could not see the delivery. Hussain stepped away and the ball narrowly missed his stumps. The English press questioned why it hadn't been called a no-ball. But South African Umpires Association chief Brian Basson confirmed that had the ball hit the stumps, even if the umpire had not seen the delivery, Hussain would have been given out, as in terms of the laws such deliveries cannot be called no-balls.

Rumours then did the rounds that the England camp would oppose my presence at the fifth Test in Centurion, but Ali Bacher immediately made it clear that the UCBSA would not change umpires during a Test series. 'He will not be the first or the last to make mistakes,' Bacher said, 'and teams have to realise that Rudi and the other umpires stand under tremendous pressure because nobody wants to walk any more [when they know they're out] and everybody's always appealing.'

As Ali Bacher had promised, I stood again in the fifth and final Test at Centurion, a match that was later to become notorious when Hansie Cronjé admitted to match fixing during the King Commission inquiry. It certainly was one of the strangest matches of my career. Rain was a nuisance on the first day, with almost one-and-a-half sessions lost as South Africa finished on 155/6. But worse was to come, as both the second and third days were rained out without a ball being bowled. The losses to the Northerns Cricket Union were later estimated at more than R2.5 million.

The main problem area was at the Hennops River end of the ground, and some suggested that the area could have been cut out and replaced with dry sods. But both Darrell Hair and I were against this. Some former English county players contended that had the game been played in England, it would have gone ahead. And a few media guys even made snide remarks about South African players, who they said had become a bit too 'prima donna' in their attitude.

When play finally resumed, South Africa managed to add 93 runs before Hansie declared, a controversial decision by all accounts. Hansie didn't have much to lose, anyway, as his side had already wrapped up the series 2-0, but I still thought to myself that he was playing Father Christmas with his declaration. At no stage, though, did I ever suspect anything like match fixing. Hansie was the last person I would have suspected of such a wicked thing. I discuss the remainder of this Test in more detail in the chapter on match fixing, but suffice it to say that England went on to win the match in the last over.

4

Put to the test:
Test highlights 2000–2005

> **❝** *Then, on 28 October, I received the ultimate accolade from the world's leading cricketers when I was voted the best umpire in the world, collecting 28 per cent of the votes, just ahead of Dave Shepherd. I have always admired Dave as an umpire and as a person, and I regarded it as a big compliment to have pipped him to the title.* **❞**

I had my first chance to stand in the Caribbean in May 2000, when I was appointed for the first and second Tests between the West Indies and Pakistan in Georgetown and Bridgetown. During these matches, I had the privilege of watching the pace duo of Curtley Ambrose and Courtney Walsh from close up. To be attacked from either side of the pitch by these two bowlers was a prospect no batsman could relish. The first Test was nevertheless a big disappointment, as it was washed out in the final two days.

The second Test was also drawn, but at least Courtney Walsh's 5/22 and Wavell Hinds's score of 165 were highlights. It was therefore down to the third and final Test to decide the series, and a 19-run last-wicket partnership between Jimmy Adams and Courtney Walsh saw the West Indies home in one of the most exciting of Test matches. In the same match, Wasim Akram showed again what a great player he was, claiming match figures of 11 wickets for 110 runs.

I was due to stand in a warm-up match in Toronto at the end of September, but one evening late in August I was driving my car in Despatch when a truck skipped a red robot – a very common occurrence in our country! – and hit me side-on. I was seriously injured, pinned behind the steering wheel, and ended up in hospital for a few weeks. That put paid to my Toronto outing. I also missed an ICC umpires meeting in London. My ribs were still sore when I eventually got onto my exercise bike and started jogging again. I have always tried to keep my back and legs strong, because those are the parts of your body that endure the most strain from six hours of umpiring on each day of a five-day Test.

By December I was fit enough for my last Test of the year, and I walked out onto St George's Park without any discomfort for the second Test between the Proteas and the Kiwis. The home side won easily by seven wickets, despite a fine 150 by Matthew Sinclair in New Zealand's first innings. The win gave South Africa a 2-0 lead in the three-match series. (For the record, the third Test was drawn.)

My first outing for 2001 was a Test in Sydney, Australia – my first umpiring visit to both the city and the continent – where I stood in the fifth West Indies/Australia Test. In their good old days, a West Indian touring team would have troubled the Australians with ferocious pace bowling and dazzling batting, but the side of 2000/01 was a mere shadow of those cavalier Caribbean teams of the past.

Led by Jimmy Adams in the battle for the Frank Worrell Trophy, the West Indians were crushed in the first Test in Brisbane inside the space of three days. They surrendered in the second Test in Perth, in the third Test in Adelaide, and suffered another heavy defeat in the fourth Test in Melbourne. I stood in the fifth Test in Sydney, and looked on as they were overpowered by Australia.

Glenn McGrath, who was the Player of the Series, had match figures of 10/27 in Brisbane, which he followed up with a stunning hat-trick in Perth, taking his 300th Test wicket. I had the privilege to be there when, some years later, he claimed his 500th scalp in Test cricket! Here was a most competitive cricketer if ever I saw one. Australian batsmen Michael Slater and the Waugh brothers were among the runs, and in their first clean sweep of a five-Test series in 69 years, the Aussies easily retained the trophy.

From Australia it was back to Centurion for the third South Africa/Sri Lanka Test. In the meantime, Shaun Pollock had taken over as captain from the disgraced Hansie Cronjé, proving that the added responsibility of captaincy was no burden to his overall game. He won the Man of the Match award with a maiden century after the Proteas had been struggling at 204/7. Pollock had by then already firmly established himself as one of the world's leading all-rounders.

From my seven Tests in 2001, the next one in Kandy, where Sri Lanka hosted England, the India/Australia clash in Chennai and the Ashes Test at The Oval (which is dealt with in the chapter on the Ashes) stood out for me. The match in Kandy, however, will be remembered for the wrong reasons and was one that any umpire would rather have missed.

When I got to Sri Lanka, the dust was just settling on the controversial first Test match in Galle, where the occasion had been soured by some dicey umpiring decisions. The press reported that England were hoping that the umpires for the second Test, Sri Lanka's BC Cooray and I, would be a big improvement on the previous game's umpires. England's Alec Stewart was calling for stronger, more experienced umpires, especially on spinning wickets, and the call to introduce neutral umpires in all Test matches as soon as possible was also repeated. Proponents of instituting neutral umpires argued that home umpires could be blamed for being biased when they made bad decisions that went against the visitors – which one can't deny is a natural reaction. In view of the controversy, match referee Hanumant Singh instructed Cooray and me to refer all debatable decisions in the upcoming Test to the third official.

Sri Lanka scored a respectable 297 in their first innings, but England did better with 387, their skipper Nasser Hussain leading the way with 109. Sri Lanka had begun the fourth day hoping to quickly wrap up the England innings, but instead England gained a lead of 90 runs. TV replays suggested that Hussain was out on 50 and 62 before he went on to his hundred, which started the unhappiness in the Sri Lankan camp. To make matters even worse, Sri Lanka lost three quick wickets in their second innings, but the controversial dismissal of Sanath Jayasuriya really caused the big stir.

Jayasuriya drove at Andrew Caddick, edging the ball into the ground (or so it later seemed). But the ball ballooned up and Graham Thorpe caught it at third slip. Cooray asked me to confirm that the catch had been taken cleanly – which I did – and he sent Jayasuriya on his way. Ironically, at an earlier ICC conference, Cooray had specifically asked permission to refer a bump catch to the television umpire, but his request was refused. The ruling stated that catches could only be referred if there was doubt as to whether the ball had been taken cleanly, but bump balls were a matter for the on-field umpires to decide for themselves.

Jayasuriya made no effort to hide his anger, only to be hauled into the match referee's office later to receive a suspension of two Test matches and two ODIs; he was also fined 60 per cent of his match fee.

In the end, Sri Lanka was dismissed for 250, leaving England a tricky target of 161. They managed it with only three wickets to spare. Sri Lanka felt the match could have – maybe *should* have – gone their way.

Watching the replays afterwards, I had to admit that my colleague and I did not have the best of umpiring days. And our mistakes were contributing to the players' already fraying tempers. Cooray, especially, was blasted by the media, and after the Test he hung up his coat after 23 years of umpiring. He admitted to the mistakes he'd made, saying it was easily the worst game he had ever had.

What had increased the pressure on both of us was the fact that the media spotlight had focused relentlessly on the umpiring after the first Test in Galle, with each decision repeatedly being examined. But at least they could not accuse us of home bias in this instance!

From the turmoil of Kandy I moved on to Chennai, where the third Test between India and Australia produced some spectacular milestones, and I thoroughly enjoyed the spectacle. Matthew Hayden blasted 203, hitting six sixes to set a new record of the most sixes by an Australian in an innings, becoming only the second batsman to hit six sixes in an innings against India after Viv Richards at Delhi in 1974/75. The big opener finished the series with 549 runs, at an average of 109.80.

During the Test, Steve Waugh was dismissed 'handled the ball', only the sixth time in Test-cricket history that this had happened. Law 33 of the Laws of Cricket dictates that a batsman is out 'handled the ball' if he wilfully touches the ball while in play with a hand or hands not holding the bat – unless he does so with the consent of the opposing side. The bowler is not credited with the wicket. It is an unusual occurrence, and usually happens because the batsman sweeps the ball away from his stumps while trying to protect his wicket.

The great Tendulkar scored his 25th Test hundred for India, playing in his 82nd Test. The Indian bowlers also contributed their share. Harbhajan Singh had match figures of 15/217, the second best by an Indian in all Tests after Narendra Hirwani's 16 for 136 against the West Indies at the same venue in 1987/88. But an even more significant statistic was that his 32 wickets out of the 50 Australian wickets represented 64 per cent of the total wickets taken by the Indian bowlers – the most dominating performance by an individual bowler ever in a Test series.

At the end of 2001, 10 seasons after my Test debut, I had 27 Test matches under my belt and I became a member of the ICC's Elite Panel of Umpires in 2002. In the next three years, until the end of 2004, I would umpire in 32 Tests, which just illustrates how much our umpiring duties have increased. In 2004 alone, I stood in 13 Tests – the most for any year of my career.

I also had a fairly busy time in 2002, standing in 10 Tests, the most for me in a year up to that stage. In early February 2002 an Australian side, led by Ricky Ponting, toured South Africa, and their line-up was surely stronger than it is today. Back then they won more than they lost. I stood in the first Test at the New Wanderers Stadium in Johannesburg, and I was privileged to witness one of the most devastating innings – if not *the* most devastating – by a batsman in my entire career. Yes, who else but Adam Gilchrist? Hitting 19 fours and eight sixes, he scored 204 not out to help Australia to an innings and 360-run win over the Proteas. The South Africans could only scrape together 159 and 133 in their two innings. Glenn McGrath (5/21) and Shane Warne (4/44) were the chief destroyers of the South African batsmen.

The indomitable Gilchrist was at it again in the second Test at Newlands, when he scored 138 not out, Australia winning by four wickets in the end. I also saw one of the saddest incidents I've witnessed in Test cricket when, in South Africa's second innings Neil McKenzie was run out with his score on 99. In pursuit of their target, Hayden with 96 and Ponting with 100 not out then saw the Aussies home. Incidentally, it was also the match that marked the debut of Graeme Smith, who went on to establish himself as one of the top batsmen in the world and a fine Proteas captain.

This Test turned out to be the last one I could officiate on home soil. The ICC had finally decided that only neutral on-field umpires would be deployed in future Tests – thereby pleasing those who had bayed for this rule to be adopted. It meant that I would never again stand in a Test played by South Africa. I suppose the ruling had to come some time or another, although I have always maintained that an umpire should be neutral and honest whether he stands in a Test at home or abroad. But at least the ICC's decision meant that no one could accuse umpires of home bias any longer. (In January 2010, the ICC announced it might do away with the concept of neutral umpires by the time the Ashes were played, as the decision review system (DRS) would clear the decks for officials to stand in matches featuring their home country.) In ODIs, the rule is one neutral and one local umpire.

I flew over to Pakistan about a month later to stand in the first and second Tests of their series against New Zealand, but only the first took place. I'll explain why in a minute. Pakistan won the first Test in Lahore by an innings and 324 runs; big Inzamam-ul-Haq scored a phenomenal 329 runs, which was quite something to behold, and their 'Rawalpindi Express', Shoaib Akhtar, took 6/11 in just over eight overs.

The Kiwis were hoping to avenge this big humiliation, but we never got as far as the second Test. On 8 May a bomb went off close to our hotel in Karachi, killing 14 people. Fortunately I was elsewhere in town at the time of the explosion, but I was shocked by the devastation that greeted me on my return to my hotel room. I will elaborate on the incident in a later chapter; suffice it to say for now that it caused chaos and the match to be called off. The players and officials packed as quickly as possible, and that same evening match referee Mike Procter (the former Springbok cricketer) and I were on our way back to South Africa.

Soon afterwards I stood in the West Indies/New Zealand series, in Bridgetown and St George's. Remarkably, the New Zealander Scott Styris, who had missed out on his debut match in Karachi because of the bomb blast, scored 107 on finally making his debut in St George's, Grenada. His 107 was only the seventh occasion on which a New Zealand batsman had scored a century on debut.

I had my second opportunity to stand at Lord's when I was appointed for the first and second Tests in the England/India five-Test series. For the record, England won the Lord's Test by 170 runs, Hussain scoring 155, while the second at Nottingham, when Michael Vaughan scored 197, was a drawn affair. The series ended all square after the fifth Test was called off due to heavy rain, but at least there was one highlight in Dravid's double hundred.

The year ended on a personal high when I officiated in three of the Ashes Tests, which I describe in a separate chapter. Then, on 28 October, I received the ultimate accolade from the world's leading cricketers when I was voted the best umpire in the world, collecting 28 per cent of the votes, just ahead of Dave Shepherd. I have always admired Dave as an umpire and as a person, and I regarded it as a big compliment to have pipped him to the title. His death in October 2009 was a sad moment for me, as I had spent many a day on the field with him.

The highlights of my 2003 season were undoubtedly the World Cup tournament in South Africa, which I discuss elsewhere, and the series between Australia and India, played in Australia. But my season kicked off umpiring in Georgetown and Port of Spain, where Ponting's boys took on the West Indies and retained the Frank Worrell Trophy, despite another wonderful Test century from Brian Lara. It was a special moment for Lara, as his century took him past Sir Gary Sobers's record for the most Test runs in the Caribbean, but I'm sure Sir Gary didn't begrudge him his milestone.

I also officiated in Ahmedabad and Mohali in India's first two Tests against New Zealand, but these produced no result and eight centuries. Cricket can take you to all corners of the world, and I also made visits to Darwin in far Northern Australia and Cairns for Australia's clash with Bangladesh. No prizes for guessing who won that one. Not often does a side win a match with scores of only 207 and 201, but Australia still won the Darwin Test by 149 runs! At the end of the year, however, a much bigger task confronted the Aussies when they faced India.

I was lucky to see an in-form Ricky Ponting scoring 242 in Adelaide, where I stood in the second Test, preceding his 257 in Melbourne, as well as Rahul Dravid's double hundred. Also in Melbourne, Virender Sehwag came close to his double century with 195, while Tendulkar scored a double century in Sydney. Considering that apart from these there were four more hundreds by Australian batsmen and three more by the Indians, it was a high-scoring affair in the four Tests, which ended in a one-all series draw.

My busiest season came in 2004, when I stood in 13 Tests in 10 months, and which took me to Sri Lanka, the West Indies, Pakistan, Zimbabwe, India, England and Australia, which was quite some travelling, believe me. My year started off with clashes between Sri Lanka and Australia in Galle and the West Indies and England in Bridgetown, after which I left for Rawalpindi, where I anticipated some fireworks between the two arch-rivals Pakistan and India in the third Test.

But it turned out to be a surprisingly one-sided contest, India scoring 600 – with Dravid contributing a big 270 – to beat Pakistan by an innings and 131 runs. With that India sealed a historic series victory in Pakistan, their first overseas series win in more than a decade. Nevertheless, I can't remember catches being dropped like they were by the Indians on the last day, one after the other – six of them in just the first 40 minutes.

Before this series, India had played 20 Tests in Pakistan, winning none. Winning the two Tests in this series, added to their performance against Australia, proved that they were once again a strong force in Test cricket.

The third of my eight Test-career appearances at Lord's followed when I handled the first of the Kiwis' four Test clashes with England. In spite of scores of 386 and 336, New Zealand still went down to the Englishmen by seven wickets. England also won the next two Tests, to take the series 3-0. The highlight for me at Lord's was South African–born Andrew Strauss's debut for England, which he celebrated by making 112. Strauss has thoroughly established himself in the side over the past years, to the extent that he now captains the team. He has also been joined in the England team by another four South African–born players: Kevin Pietersen, Matthew Prior, Jonathan Trott and Craig Kieswetter. Just think what depth South Africa would have had today with those five!

I was back at Lord's barely two months later, where England hosted the West Indies in the first Test for the Wisden Trophy. England dominated the series: they won the first Test by 210 runs, Strauss once again scoring a century; the second by 256 runs; the third by seven wickets; and the final Test at The Oval, where I umpired again, by 10 wickets.

During the last months of the year I had plenty of opportunity to watch the formidable Australians play, first in their four-Test series in India and then on their home grounds against Pakistan. The Aussies took the first match in Bangalore comfortably, but the second in Chennai, where I stood, was drawn. They won the third Test by more than 300 runs, then lost the fourth in Mumbai (which I also umpired) by only 13 runs. Their second-innings total of only 93 was the worst I've ever seen of them.

I finished 2004 with the three-Test Australia/Pakistan series, which the Aussies dominated and eventually clinched 3-0. I handled the first Test in Perth, which Australia won by a massive 491 runs, as well as the second Test in Melbourne, which they won by nine wickets. In Melbourne, Pakistan had the better of the exchanges on the first couple of days, but Damien Martyn's outstanding century turned the game on its head. The series was concluded in Sydney in early 2005, when Ponting's men again won by nine wickets. Ponting top-scored in the series with just over 400 runs, which included a double century; he was followed by Justin Langer with 390 and Damien Martyn with 310.

As you can imagine, there are few dull moments when these two sides go into battle against each other. In Perth, Shoaib Akhtar was fined 40 per cent of his match fee after the match umpires (Billy Bowden, Steve Davis and I) charged him with Level 1 misconduct. He had trapped Hayden lbw and then pointed him towards the dressing room with both fingers – not just once, but three times. The ICC Code says that a member of the fielding side may not engage in 'pointing or gesturing towards the pavilion in an aggressive manner ... upon the dismissal of a batsman' – which was exactly what Ahktar had done.

We also saw some fiery exchanges in Melbourne between Ahktar and Justin Langer, at a stage when Ahktar had removed Hayden, Ponting and Darren Lehmann cheaply, and Langer had to lead a fightback. Ahktar was at his quickest and most aggressive, and Langer had just escaped a bouncer from Ahktar when the very next badly bruised his hand. Predictably batsman and bowler had a few harsh words to say to each other, so much so that we as the umpires, as well as Pakistan captain Yousuf Youhana, had to calm down tempers.

I told Langer to cool it, but he replied that he wasn't being malicious – it was just a bit of 'psychological warfare'. He told the press afterwards that Ahktar had been the quickest man he'd ever faced, and that to him it was one of the greatest duels in cricket to bat against him. And it's also something to behold from behind the stumps, I can tell you.

At the end of 2004, the world was shocked by the news of the devastating tsunami that had hit South-East Asia. At short notice, the ICC organised a one-day charity match in Melbourne in aid of the victims. The match, played on 10 January 2005, involved a World XI vs an Asian XI, and it featured some of the world's top players. So it was an honour for me to be appointed to stand as on-field umpire, along with Billy Bowden.

The year held a career highlight for me when I stood in three Tests of the 2005 Ashes series, played in England. It was a great series and a wonderful privilege to have been part of it, but more about that in the chapters on the Ashes. For the rest of the year, I travelled to India, Australasia and Pakistan, following the charity match in Melbourne with the first India/Pakistan Test in Mohali. It was a high-scoring match and, not surprisingly, drawn; in fact, it was a high-scoring series, India and Pakistan winning a Test apiece for a series draw.

It's not often that a bowler gets fined for excessive appealing, but this happened to India's paceman Lakshmipathy Balaji, at Mohali. Ironically, he recorded a career best of 9/171, but it took the gloss off somewhat when he was fined 30 per cent of his match fee after the game. It was his first match for India in nearly a year, so perhaps he was just being overly enthusiastic, but Darrell Hair and I felt he was overdoing the appealing, and match referee Chris Broad agreed.

I umpired in the last two Tests of Australia's tour to New Zealand, a series dominated 2-0 by the visitors. It was again a joy to watch Gilchrist hammering the bowlers, top-scoring the series with 343 runs and a highest score of 162. Shane Warne was at his best again in the first Test in Christchurch, claiming 5/39 in one innings.

Following the Ashes series, I was privileged to see most of the world's best cricketers together when I stood in the Aussies' Super Test against the World XI at the Sydney Cricket Ground (SCG). The Australians, on a mission to compensate for their Ashes defeat, beat the World XI by 210 runs. Warne and Stuart MacGill (what a pity he didn't have more opportunities for Australia) bowled superbly, demolishing the World XI, a side that included fine batsmen like Brian Lara, Rahul Dravid, Jacques Kallis, Inzamam-ul-Haq, Andrew Flintoff and Mark Boucher.

A short time later I watched Australia massacre the West Indies in Brisbane and Hobart. They won the first Test by 379 runs and the second by nine wickets; the third, which I didn't umpire, they won by seven wickets. The highest scores were recorded by Brian Lara, with 226, and Ricky Ponting, with 146 in Brisbane; the dependable Mike Hussey also weighed in with two hundreds.

Showing great footwork as usual, Lara was unbeaten at close on the third day, after becoming Test cricket's second-highest run-scorer, passing Steve Waugh's tally of 10 927 when he was on 12 runs. I gave him out next morning caught behind to Warne, but afterwards it seemed that his bat had missed the ball and brushed his pad instead. In Brisbane, Brett Lee was as fiery as usual and took 5/30. His 18 wickets were the most for the series.

I had a final appearance in 2005 in Lahore, where Pakistan crushed England by an innings and 100 runs. The highlight was Mohammad Yousuf's 223 and Kamran Akmal's 154 in their massive first-innings total of 636 runs. That brought to an end a very demanding four years of umpiring and travelling for me – 42 Test matches in four years.

5

Tested to the limit:
Test highlights 2006–2009

" *I thought he had nicked the ball and gave him out. After the match, I apologised to Sangakkara. It's never pleasant to know that you have unfairly deprived a player of a possible seventh double century and the distinction of being the first man ever to reach 200 in three successive Tests.* **"**

My Test-umpiring schedule didn't become any easier between 2006 and 2009. I stood in 32 matches, of which 13 took place in 2009. I guess I couldn't complain, because at least it helped me to reach my target of 100 Tests more quickly. It started with two demanding appearances in India, where the home side took on Pakistan. I had to stand in the first Test in Lahore and the second Test in Faisalabad. The match in Lahore was drawn after Pakistan scored 679 and India 410/1 – it's obvious that batsmen dominated!

In the series, Younis Khan (553, HS 199), Mohammad Yousuf (461, HS 173) and Shahid Afridi (330, HS 156), all three from Pakistan, made the most runs, but India's Sehwag recorded the highest individual score with 254 runs. One had to feel sorry for poor Younis Khan. He had missed a double century in consecutive Tests – after scoring 199 in the first Test in Lahore, he lost his wicket in the second Test on 194!

I was supposed to stand in the second Test in Faisalabad with Darrell Hair, but before the start of the series, the Pakistan Cricket Board (PCB) had considered asking the ICC to replace Hair for the final two Tests against India. To be honest, relations between Darrell and Pakistan had never been great, and things would come to a head the following year at The Oval in the fourth Test between England and Pakistan.

In that match, Hair accused Pakistan of ball tampering and penalised them by five runs, with the result that Pakistan refused to play after tea. In the end, the match was awarded to England. But more about that later in the chapter.

Whatever had happened in the meantime, the fact of the matter was that I stood in Faisalabad not with Hair, but with Simon Taufel. It was another batsman-dominated game, and it petered out into a rather boring display on the last day. At the tea interval, when it was already clear that the game was going nowhere, Simon Taufel and I spoke to both Inzamam-ul-Haq and Rahul Dravid, the two captains, who both agreed to call off the match at that point. The match referee, Ranjan Madugalle, however, was unable to stop the match, as the laws did not allow for such an event. Madugalle therefore had to ask the two teams to go through the motions until only eight overs remained in the game.

This incidence just proved to me again that a change in the laws is required. If a result is not likely on the final day of a Test, it should be possible to call off the game. I don't think there's anything wrong if the ICC changes the laws to allow a Test match to be called off at tea on the last day – with the consent of both captains, of course.

Later in the year I umpired in Auckland, where the Kiwis hosted the West Indies, and in Colombo, where Sri Lanka hosted Pakistan. I also had another stint at Lord's, where England played Sri Lanka, and finished the series in the third Test in Nottingham. After the drawn Test at Lord's, the home side gained the advantage in Birmingham, where they beat the Sri Lankans by six wickets.

But then they lost by 134 runs in the final Test in Nottingham for a one-all series draw. Kevin Pietersen was the series' top scorer with 360 runs, which included a knock of 158. His previous century, that famous one at The Oval in the Ashes the year before (see Chapter 6) – and which I was honoured to watch from behind the stumps – was also worth exactly 158, but I doubt that the one against Sri Lanka would have been as precious to him.

For me, the year finished with three Tests in the one-sided Ashes series, but before I could get excited about that, I had to stand in two matches in the four-Test West Indies/India series in the Caribbean. India eventually won the series 1-0, after clinching the final Test by 47 runs in Kingston. Wasim Jaffer top-scored with 212 at St John's, but there were also another seven centuries scored during the series – three of them at Basseterre, by Daren Ganga, Ramnaresh Sarwan and VVS Laxman.

A little less than a year later, in 2007, I again umpired the West Indies, this time getting well beaten by England, who had returned home from Australia earlier following a crushing series defeat. I was back at Lord's for the first Test of the four-Test series, and I also stood in the second Test in Leeds. While the first Test was drawn, England won the next three for a 3-0 series win, taking the second Test at Leeds by an innings and 283 runs. There I was fortunate to see Kevin Pietersen smash his highest Test score yet of 226. He's not the most stylish of batsmen I've ever seen, but, boy, is he effective! I know there are many people at home – especially in Cricket SA – who pretend that his move to England was no real loss, but I'm sure there are times when they would love to have him in their ranks.

The year 2007 was, of course, dominated by the controversial events at the Cricket World Cup in the West Indies, of which I had been an integral part. But I was also dragged into the Darrell Hair/ICC legal case. The events of the World Cup are covered in another chapter, but I will elaborate here on the Darrell Hair saga.

At a London tribunal in early October 2007, Hair caused a stir when he alleged that I had called the Pakistan players 'cheats' in a phone conversation we'd had during the World Cup. At the time, he was suing his employers, the ICC, for having unfairly removed him from their international panel, allegedly on the basis of racial discrimination.

In August the previous year, when England played Pakistan at The Oval, five penalty runs were awarded to England during the game when Hair signalled to the umpires that Pakistan had tampered with the ball. An early tea was taken, but Pakistan staged a protest after the interval and refused to continue playing. Hair, his colleague Billy Doctrove and the two England batsmen walked out alone and waited for 15 minutes before the covers were brought on, signalling the end of play.

Pakistan eventually did make it out onto the field, but by that stage Hair and Doctrove had already decided to award the match to England – which, according to the laws of the game, was not out of order. Law 21.3 says: 'In the opinion of the umpires, if a team refuses to play, the umpires shall award the match to the other side.' So England won the match, and in the following days it became clear that Hair's position was becoming increasingly untenable as the Asian bloc applied pressure on the ICC.

Bob Woolmer, then coach of Pakistan, and team manager Zaheer Abbas both insisted their side had not been guilty of tampering with the ball, but the ICC nevertheless charged Inzamam with ball tampering and bringing the game into disrepute. Eventually, however, the Pakistan team was cleared of the charge, the verdict being that 'the marks were as consistent with normal wear and tear, and with the ball being pitched into the rough and contact with cricket equipment, as they are with deliberate human intervention'.

At the same time, the Pakistan Cricket Board said that it no longer wanted Hair to officiate in any of its team's matches, and in November he was banned from umpiring in internationals. The Asian bloc had voted for his removal, even though England, Australia and New Zealand had wanted him to stay. Billy Doctrove's career was not affected.

But Hair was not going to take the ICC's decision lying down. Three months later, in February 2007, he instructed his lawyers to issue an application alleging racial discrimination to the London Central Employment Tribunal. He claimed that 'if I had been from West Indies or Pakistan or India, I might have been treated differently, like Doctrove'. He also bemoaned the fact that he had lost around US$3.4 million in earnings through the ICC's action. His Queen's Counsel (QC) told the hearing that his client 'was treated the way he was because the ICC bowed to the racially discriminatory pressure that was brought to bear on it by the Asian bloc and ICC board member supporters … [T]he Asian bloc is dominant in cricket, sometimes it uses that dominance inappropriately. Everyone knows it, but most are afraid to say so.'

On the second day of the hearing, things took a nasty turn when Hair claimed I had called the Pakistanis 'cheats'. The phone conversation in which I was supposed to have said this apparently happened after Ireland had eliminated Pakistan from the World Cup. I was quoted as saying, 'That's great news. Those cheats can now go home.' You can just imagine what a difficult situation I was placed in by the allegation. Suddenly an obviously bitter Hair had brought my umpiring impartiality and reputation under suspicion.

But Michael Beloff QC, the ICC's barrister, dismissed Hair's claim, saying, 'It's sheer mudslinging. What you were hoping to do was cause the ICC maximum embarrassment and cajole them into making some sort of offer to you.'

Hair had offered to leave in August 2006, but only if he was paid $500 000. The ICC defended him, stating that 'Hair was under great stress when he wrote these letters [demanding the money]. Darrell had no dishonest, underhand or malicious intent. He was seeking a solution.' When Hair unconditionally dropped all charges against the ICC on 9 October 2007, the ICC announced that he had undertaken to work with their management in a rehabilitation programme over the next six months and that the ICC board would meet in March to discuss the results and decide whether he could return to elite umpiring, and on what terms.

In a way Darrell Hair had the last laugh when, in March 2008, the ICC restored him to the Elite Panel. He stood in the England vs New Zealand Tests in May/June 2008 at Old Trafford and Trent Bridge. His contract with the ICC expired in March 2009.

So Darrell's life went on, but obviously the Pakistan Cricket Board was furious over his allegation that I had called the Pakistanis cheats. The chairman of the Pakistan Cricket Board, Nasim Ashraf, wrote to the ICC, requesting an inquiry into the allegations made against me. In my job, I talk to a lot of people a lot of the time, and I recall talking to Hair during the World Cup, but certainly not that I had made the 'cheats' remark.

In November/December 2007 I stood in two of the India vs Pakistan Tests – in Kolkata and Bangalore – and before the series I sought out the Pakistan players and made it clear to them that I had never called them cheats, as Darrell Hair had claimed. They accepted me at my word and we got along very well throughout the series.

The whole Darrell Hair incident was unfortunate and both Hair and the ICC suffered some damage to their image. Some believe that the ICC treated him poorly, and that they should have lent him more support when the Asian bloc called for his head.

The last two months of 2007 were fairly busy for me, as I was standing in both of the Tests in the Australia/Sri Lanka series, as well as in the India/Pakistan series in India. Australia took the series against Sri Lanka 2-0, winning the first Test in Brisbane by an innings and 40 runs. Michael Clarke, Mike Hussey and Phil Jaques scored centuries for the Aussies, which Hussey and Jaques followed up with another century apiece in the second Test in Hobart. Brett Lee bowled superbly throughout the series and won the Player of the Series award: he took 4/26 and 4/86 in Brisbane and 4/82 and 4/87 in Hobart.

The Hobart Test, which Australia won by 96 runs, wasn't without controversy. My decision to give out Kumar Sangakkara on 192 became the talking point of the match. He had swung at a rising delivery from Stuart Clark and was caught by Ponting in the slips. I thought he had nicked the ball and gave him out. The replays, however, showed that the ball had deflected from his shoulder. After the match, I apologised to him. It's never pleasant to know that you have unfairly deprived a player of a possible seventh double century and the distinction of being the first man ever to reach 200 in three successive Tests. Sangakkara's innings was nevertheless the highest a Sri Lankan had ever scored in Australia, surpassing Aravinda de Silva's 167 in Brisbane in 1989.

The Test was also an exceptional milestone for one of my favourite batsmen, Adam Gilchrist, who became the first player to hit 100 sixes in Tests – wasn't he always destined for that record? The hundredth six came off Muralitharan, of all people, and landed outside the ground, where a bloke in a red jacket pounced on it. Gillie made it known that he would love to keep that specific ball, and the whole cricket world was happy for him when it was indeed returned for his trophy cabinet at home.

The end of the series also marked the launch of the Warne-Muralitharan Trophy, named in their honour for future Tests between Australia and Sri Lanka. At the time, some robust verbal exchanges between the two were published in the newspapers, but on the day the trophy was launched it was all dismissed as a 'misunderstanding'.

I was withdrawn at short notice from the forthcoming Test series between Sri Lanka and England. According to malicious rumours that were doing the rounds, I had been withdrawn because Sri Lanka was unhappy about the Sangakkara incident.

But there was a perfectly good explanation. Billy Bowden, who would have stood in the India/Pakistan series, had to undergo an operation, with Steve Bucknor replacing him. But Steve didn't have his passport ready, and as I was the only umpire whose passport was in order, we were swapped around.

I finished the year with two demanding Tests between Pakistan and India in India, officiating in the second (Kolkata) and third (Bangalore) Tests. India had won the first Test. The match in Kolkata was drawn, following some big scores. India made 616/5 in their first innings, Jaffer scoring 202, Ganguly 102 and Laxman 112 not out. In Pakistan's first innings, Misbah-ul-Haq made 161 not out and Akmal 119 in a total of 456. India declared on 184/4, leaving Pakistan a target of 345. But with Pakistan on 214/4, and Younis Khan on 107 not out, the match ended in a draw.

The third Test in Bangalore was also drawn, giving India a 1-0 series win. The highlight of the Test was Ganguly's knock of 239, his highest-ever Test score. Yuvraj Singh scored 169 and Irfan Pathan also weighed in with a century for a big first-innings total of 626. Pakistan replied with 537, Misbah-ul-Haq scoring another century following his 169 in the first innings. Chasing a target of 374, Pakistan were in trouble on 162/7, but hung on for a draw. Predictably, Ganguly was named Player of the Series.

That brought down the curtain on an eventful 2007 for me. At least it was the first time in five years that I could spend Christmas at home, believe it or not. I already had 87 Test matches under my belt, and I had time to speculate on how long it was going to take me to reach my goal of 100 Test matches. My guess was that it would be in another two years' time.

The biggest series that awaited me in 2008 was Australia's tour of India. These matches have always produced good drama, and it was to be no different this time round. Before then, however, I had commitments in New Zealand, where England toured, and in Sri Lanka, who hosted India.

England clinched the series in New Zealand 2-1. Andrew

Strauss, with a fine 177, and Kevin Pietersen, with 129, produced the goods to set England on course for the series win. In the Sri Lanka/India series, Sri Lanka took the series honours 2-1 from three matches. I umpired in the second Test in Galle, where India won by 170 runs, and in the third and final Test in Colombo, at the Pakiosothy Saravanamuttu Stadium (PSS), when the home side clinched the series with an eight-wicket victory. In Galle, Sehwag scored 201 not out, and in Colombo, Sangakkara (at the PSS), Jayawardene, Thilan Samaraweera, Tillakaratne Dilshan and Malinda Warnapura (at the SSC) all contributed centuries.

Australia was scheduled to tour India in October, and the ICC wanted to ensure that the series would be free of any acrimony. Earlier in the year, India had agreed to continue their tour of Australia only after the ICC had pacified them by withdrawing Steve Bucknor from the forthcoming Test in Perth. Bucknor and Mark Benson had umpired in the Sydney Test, which had been marked by a number of controversial decisions, especially from Bucknor.

As a result, the ICC decided to exclude Bucknor and Benson from the India games, and I was appointed along with Asad Rauf of Pakistan to take care of the first two Tests in Bangalore and Mohali. Billy Bowden and Aleem Dar would stand in the last two Tests in New Delhi and Nagpur.

India eventually won the series 2-0. It was strange to see Australia not winning a Test in a four-match series. In Bangalore the teams played to a tame draw, although Australia looked the better side. In the second Test in Mohali, the Aussies were comprehensively outplayed, losing by 320 runs. India gathered solid scores of 469 and 314/3 declared, while Australia was disappointing with 268 and 195 (after being 58/5). It was their worst defeat in a decade. After the match, Mahendra Dhoni, the stand-in captain for India, said that he'd never seen Australia so outplayed, and even Ponting had to concede that it had probably been his worst game as captain of Australia.

The players had a lot to say in some heated exchanges during the match, and Asad Rauf and I had to intervene on a number of occasions to call for calm. Harbhajan Singh, particularly, got quite excited, and Zaheer Khan was later fined 80 per cent of his match fee for a so-called Level 2 offence, following his celebration after the dismissal of Matthew Hayden in Australia's second innings. When Hayden was adjudged lbw to Singh, Khan had 'circled the batsman and shouted at him in an aggressive manner', according to the charge laid against him. I was standing at square leg, and walking off after his dismissal, Hayden complained to me. His dismissal sparked Australia's collapse, as they lost five wickets for nine runs to slump to 58/5.

Match referee Chris Broad had no hesitation in imposing Khan's fine, saying that his behaviour was unacceptable at any level of cricket and showed a lack of respect for the batsman concerned. 'Respect for the opposition was something that we talked about in the pre-series meeting I had with both captains, and so it was disappointing that Zaheer behaved in this way,' Broad said.

In the third Test at Delhi, VVS Laxman and Gautam Gambhir both scored double centuries in India's big first-innings total of 613/7, and when Australia replied with 577, a draw was always on the cards. India went on to win the final Test in Nagpur by 172 runs to take the series 2-0.

At the end of 2008, I was appointed to stand in the Trans-Tasman Trophy two-Test series between the Aussies and their neighbours, New Zealand, in Australia. I stood with Billy Doctrove of the West Indies in the first Test in Brisbane, as well as in the second Test in Adelaide. The Brisbane Test was a bit ordinary, with Australia winning comfortably. They had scored only 214 runs in their first innings, but New Zealand replied with even less – 156. In their second outing, Simon Katich helped Australia to 268 with 131 not out. Set a target of 327 runs, the Kiwis only managed 177 in about 55 overs.

The second Test in Adelaide had more batting action. Brad Haddin had a wonderful knock of 169 in Australia's first innings of 535 in reply to New Zealand's 270. Haddin is no Adam Gilchrist yet – will anyone ever be? – but, boy, does he get on with it quickly! When he's on song, he's a joy to watch. Michael Clarke again showed he had developed into a fine cricketer by hitting 110. The Kiwis could only scrape together 203 runs, and in the end Ponting's boys won by an innings and 62 runs, taking the series 2-0.

From Australia it was across the Tasman Sea to Napier, where I stood in a New Zealand vs West Indies Test, which started on 19 December. It meant that I would again not be home for Christmas – but that was nothing unusual. In the first Test in Dunedin, the second and last days were completely washed out, and the temperature hovered around 14° C and lower. Fortunately for me I was the TV umpire, and thus a lot cosier than the poor on-field umpires!

I had to be on my toes, nevertheless, as the second Test was part of an ICC experiment in which teams could refer on-field decisions to the TV umpire for consideration. In the end, I had to look at seven referrals, of which four were reversed and three upheld. West Indies skipper Chris Gayle later said he was 'not really a big fan' of the system, and I'm sure there were a lot of other people who shared his feelings.

In Napier, where I umpired on-field, Shivnarine Chanderpaul scored his 20th Test century, and for New Zealand, Tim McIntosh notched up his first Test century. Fidel Edwards was in fine form with the ball, taking seven wickets for 87, his best figures in Tests. In the West Indies' second innings, Gayle reached his eighth century – one would have thought there had been many more! – which was his first since his devastating knock of 317 against South Africa in 2005. He looked certain to reach 200, but sadly fell short by three runs. A draw was inevitable and the series left tied at 0-0.

My 2009 commitments started with the Wisden Trophy series in the West Indies, where the local side had to face England. I have seen some poor fields in my time, but what we saw over there in February was shocking. I had to stand in the Tests in Kingston and was scheduled as TV umpire for the North Sound Test in Antigua, but it turned out to be a bit of a chaotic affair, especially in Antigua.

Things started off on a very bad note for England in the first test at Sabina Park in Kingston, when they lost the match by an innings and 23 runs. England hadn't done too badly in reaching 318 in their first innings, Kevin Pietersen contributing 97 runs. Even when the West Indies replied in their first innings with a total of 392, with Sarwan and Gayle contributing centuries, it didn't seem like the end of the world for Andrew Strauss and his men. But then England went in to bat again, their goal being to knock off the deficit of 74. What followed was unbelievable.

I saw one Englishman after the other disappear before my eyes as Jerome Taylor ripped through them, taking 5/11 in nine overs. He attacked the stumps relentlessly, but in England's defence, there were definite signs of uneven bounce. England was finally bundled out for a mere 51 runs, 23 short of making the West Indies bat again. Someone pointed out that, ironically, five years before, Englishman Steve Harmison had taken 7/12 on the same wicket.

One would have thought that this was England's lowest Test total ever, but it is, in fact, their third lowest, the worst being the 45 runs they scored in 1887 against Australia. And it wasn't their lowest total in the West Indies either – as recently as 1994, they were skittled for only 46 in Port of Spain. But in Kingston, when they were 26/7 at one stage, even that score looked well beyond them.

The second Test was to be contested at the Sir Vivian Richards Stadium in Antigua, and already on the eve of the Test ICC match referee Alan Hurst declared the outfield to be 'unsatisfactory'. He added that it would be impossible to know how bad the situation was until play actually got underway.

The Sir Vivian Richards Stadium was one of the expensive new arenas erected for the 2007 World Cup, but it has been beset with problems. Against local advice, it was sited in a basin near a watercourse, and in spite of installing an elaborate drainage system, sections of the outfield could still become a bog after overnight rain. In 2008 a full day's play in the West Indies/Australia Test was lost because of this, despite hot, sunny weather.

The day of the Test arrived. Chris Gayle won the toss and Jerome Taylor opened the bowling. But he failed to deliver his first ball at the first attempt, and then sent it down from parallel with the stumps after completely losing his run-up. Fidel Edwards from the other end bowled two balls before a light shower caused the players to leave the field. When play resumed, one could clearly see how the sand kicked up as Edwards ran to the crease, and he managed to bowl only two more deliveries before giving up. The captains, Chris Gayle and Andrew Strauss, and the on-field umpires, Daryl Harper and Tony Hill, and Alan Hurst discussed the situation. The run-ups were hastily dug up straight after the close, but it became clear that the only option was an outright abandonment of the match.

The situation was reminiscent of the Sabina Park disaster in 1997/98, when the match was abandoned because of a dangerous pitch after only 10.1 overs. The Test in the Sir Vivian Richards Stadium was even shorter.

Interestingly, the well-known Tony Cozier, who has commented on Caribbean cricket for almost 50 years, blamed the fiasco on the administrators, who, he said, were interested only in 'protecting their own fiefdom' and had little background in the game. He pointed out that only Wes Hall among the five consecutive presidents of the West Indies Cricket Board (WICB) over the past 20 years had been a former Test player, and that none of the six CEOs had even been reputable club cricketers.

The episode was embarrassing to the West Indian team and their local fans, and put a damper on the glory of their Kingston victory.

As a direct consequence, the third Test was moved to the island's original venue, the old Antigua Recreation Ground in St John's. Although the possibility of shifting the match to Sir Allen Stanford's private ground near the airport had been mentioned, the relationship between Stanford (who would be arrested for fraud in February 2009) and the WICB was not too great and this option was never seriously considered. Umpire Tony Hill had by then gone home, and for the third Test I took over as on-field umpire with Daryl Harper.

In the third Test, England scored 566 and 221/8 in their respective innings. This time England's performance was much improved from what I'd seen in Kingston, and both Strauss and Paul Collingwood scored centuries. The West Indies were in trouble after scoring 285 in their first innings, and having to chase a target of 503 runs, they nevertheless managed to hold on for a draw.

The fourth and fifth Tests were both drawn, the West Indies thus winning the series 1-0. The fourth Test in Bridgetown, especially, was a massive scoring affair, with England amassing 600 runs (Strauss and Ravi Bopara both scoring centuries), to which the West Indies replied with 749! Sarwan alone scored 291; Denesh Ramdin weighed in with 166.

In the meantime I headed home, as my next Tests were only scheduled for July 2009. But those Tests being part of the Ashes, I was already looking forward to them. On top of that, I was also going to notch up my 100th Test during the series – at Lord's of all places!

6

Clashes for the Ashes

" In the week leading up to the first Test, chats in the pubs, in the shops, and on the buses and trains were mostly about the Ashes, and the fans couldn't wait for the series to begin. There was an electric atmosphere at Lord's as, under cloudy skies, I strode out onto the field with Aleem Dar. "

In the history of the game, the big clashes that have stirred the most emotion and garnered the widest publicity throughout the world have always been those between the two great arch-rivals, Australia and England. For the Englishman and the Australian, there's nothing bigger or better than the Ashes. To anyone from outside these two countries, like me, these clashes for the Ashes are something special to experience.

For readers who are not familiar with the origin of the Ashes, the series dates back to 1882 and is currently played biennially, alternating between the United Kingdom and Australia. It was named after a satirical obituary published in a British newspaper in 1882 after a match at The Oval in which Australia beat England on English soil for the first time. The obituary read that English cricket had died, and that 'the body will be cremated and the ashes taken to Australia'.

The English media then referred to the subsequent tour to

Australia as 'the quest to regain The Ashes'. During that tour, a group of women from Melbourne presented the England captain with a small terracotta urn, reputedly containing the ashes of a piece of cricket equipment. The urn is not, however, the actual trophy of the Ashes series; the urn normally remains in the Marylebone Cricket Club Museum at Lord's. However, it is one of the objects a cricket fanatic simply has to go and gawk at when he's at the venue. A Waterford Crystal replica of the urn has been presented to the winners of an Ashes series since 1998/99.

In the game of rugby, the sport many of us grow up with in South Africa, the really big contest has always been South Africa versus New Zealand. Although the Australian media may suggest that nowadays there's nothing bigger than a Kiwi/Aussie test, pointing to the huge attendance figures to try to make their point, let's not kid ourselves: since facing each other for the first time in 1921, it has been the contest between the All Blacks and the Springboks that has gripped the imagination of the world's rugby fans.

I had first heard about the Ashes in my very earliest years as a cricket fanatic. I was familiar with all the names of the great legends in the series: Sir Donald Bradman, Richie Benaud, Geoff Boycott, Tony Greig, Ian Botham, the Chappell brothers. Greig would belt a bowler to the boundary and then gleefully signal his own four along with the umpire (I don't think that would be allowed today!). Of course, as a patriot, I was emotionally tied to my South African heroes – Colin Bland (I have always admired a great fielder – it was the best aspect of my own humble career!), Graeme Pollock and Barry Richards, to name but a few.

Television was only introduced to South Africa in 1976, so at school we never had a chance to watch the game on the screen. But it didn't prevent me from reading admiringly about the great stars of England and Australia. Little could I have guessed that one day I would be standing in some of the most hard-fought and exciting series of the Ashes.

The very first time I stood in a Test involving Australia was in March 1997, on my home ground of Port Elizabeth, when the Aussies played Hansie Cronjé's South African side, and the first time I stood in a Test with England playing was only in 1999, seven years after my Test debut. They were facing New Zealand, and to me it was a great occasion, as the match was being played at the hallowed ground of Lord's, the home of cricket. I knew at the time that only the top umpires had the honour of standing in the Big One between England and Australia, but I knew my time would come, even though I would have to wait a few more years for it.

The big day finally arrived on 30 August 2001, when I was standing in a full-blooded England/Australia Test at The Oval. It was the fifth Test of the series, and I consulted the record books to find that it was the 301st Test between these two sides. At the time, Australia led the victory stakes by 121 matches to England's 94. The other 86, of course, were drawn. Another interesting statistic: Of the 33 Tests played at The Oval between these two rivals, England had won 15 and Australia 6.

On a personal level, it was my 26th Test match, so I felt experienced enough for the occasion; the other umpire was Peter Willey.

At the time, Australia was already 3-1 up in the series. They had won the first Test in Birmingham by an innings and 118 runs, when Adam Gilchrist scored a career best of 152, taking 22 off Mark Butcher in a single over! In the next clash, at Lord's, the Aussies again won easily, this time by eight wickets. Mark Waugh led with a century. The third Test was a strange affair, as neither side could reach 200 runs in any innings, but Steve Waugh's men still won by seven wickets.

England finally tasted victory, by six wickets, in the fourth Test, when it was already too late. They did well after trailing by more than a hundred runs after the first innings, when centuries by Ricky Ponting and Damien Martyn gave Australia a total of 447.

Set a target of 315 in their second innings, Butcher saw them home with a gutsy 173.

So, in the fifth and final Test there was nothing for England to play for but pride, but the Aussies still rubbed it in with an innings and 25-run victory. It was the first time in Test cricket that I saw two brothers score a century each in the same innings, when Mark Waugh (120) and Steve Waugh (157) helped Australia to a big first-innings total of 641. In fact, Steve Waugh reached a milestone with his 27th Test century, moving into third place among the leading Test centurions, behind Indian Sunil Gavaskar (34) and Don Bradman (29). Trailing by just over 200, thanks to a century by Mark Ramprakash, England still found the target too much and collapsed to 184 all out.

The Australian bowlers had played more than their part in the series victory. Back in 2001, Australia had the likes of Glenn McGrath, Jason Gillespie and Shane Warne to count on, and McGrath finished the series with 32 wickets. Shane Warne had two great spells of 6/33 at Trent Bridge and 7/165 at The Oval, where I had all the time in the world to watch him weave his spinning magic. He also reached a special milestone, becoming the first spinner and only the sixth bowler to take 400 Test wickets. At the time, Courtney Walsh (519) was the leading wicket-taker. It took Warne only 92 Tests to reach this landmark, which was not as quickly as the great Richard Hadlee, who had reached 400 scalps after only 80 Tests!

A little more than a year later I was much more involved in the umpiring of the Ashes when I stood in the first three of the five Tests. This time round they fought it out Down Under, and with home-ground advantage, the Aussies were obviously the favourites.

Australia won the first Test in Brisbane convincingly by 384 runs. I saw Matthew Hayden at his best, scoring 197 in his first innings and 103 in the second, while Ponting also knocked up a century. England were woeful in their second innings, collapsing for a mere 79 runs. Who else but McGrath (4/36) and Warne (2/29) as chief destroyers?

Adelaide was even worse for England, hammered as they were by an innings and 51 runs. They started off well enough, though, Michael Vaughan hitting 177 to steer them to a decent total of 342. But the home side knocked up 552 in their first outing, Ponting scoring 154. Succumbing for only 159 in their second innings, England were still 51 runs short of making the Aussies bat again.

In Perth, where I stood in the third Test, the situation was very similar; this time, Australia won by an innings and 48 runs. Oddly, while they scored a solid first-innings total of 456, there were no centuries among the Aussie batsmen. With poor scores of 185 and 223, England was never in the game.

By winning the first three Tests, Australia ensured that they would retain the Ashes. And they were at the top of their game from the outset. A measure of the ruthlessness and efficiency of the Aussies was illustrated by the fact that in those first three Tests, the series saw only 11 of the scheduled 15 days.

Having already lost the series, it was always going to be difficult for the English to pick themselves up to avoid a 0-5 whitewash.

In the fourth Test, Australia kept tightening the screws on England, eventually winning by five wickets. The match was highlighted by Justin Langer's 250, the highest individual score of the series; Hayden also knocked up a hundred. Most people expected the worst for the final Test, but at least England saved some face by unexpectedly winning by 225 runs. Vaughan recorded England's highest individual score for the series with a well-played 183, while Butcher also added a century. Centuries by Steve Waugh and Gilchrist weren't enough to save Australia this time. When all was said and done, though, a 1-4 series defeat was humiliating for England.

My next chance to stand in the Ashes came in 2005, when the Aussies had to defend the trophy in England. Again I had the privilege of standing in the first two Tests, at Lord's and Edgbaston, Birmingham, respectively, as well as in the fifth and final Test at The Oval. Some – the English media in particular – have labelled the Test in Edgbaston as 'the greatest Test of all time', which is quite a claim! And the great Richie Benaud, who had been commentating for Australian TV for a few decades at the time, said that, from a spectator's point of view, the 2005 Ashes series ranked as the best he had seen. So I must say that I felt quite privileged to have been part of it all.

In the week leading up to the first Test, chats in the pubs, in the shops, and on the buses and trains were mostly about the Ashes, and the fans couldn't wait for the series to begin. There was an electric atmosphere at Lord's as, under cloudy skies, I strode out onto the field with Aleem Dar, followed by Michael Vaughan and the England players, and the two Australian openers, Justin Langer and Matthew Hayden.

England fans celebrated as Hayden, Ponting, Martyn and Michael Clarke went cheaply, and at 4/66, then 5/87 and 6/126, things looked pretty bad for the Aussies. Langer stuck around for a top score of 40, but they were all gone for 190, with Steve Harmison on fire with figures of 5/43. The England first-innings scorecard, however, looked even more woeful. Glenn McGrath, especially, was devastating, taking the first four wickets as well as the sixth; Marcus Trescothick, Strauss, Vaughan and Ian Bell went for 4, 2, 3 and 6 respectively, and Flintoff for a duck. The England fans couldn't believe their eyes. With their team at 21/5, 79/6 and 92/7, they were dumbstruck. Fortunately for them, Kevin Pietersen – who was making his Test debut – and Geraint Jones put up some resistance, and with Pietersen adding 57, England managed to scrape together 155.

Australia fared much better in their second innings, putting together 384, with Michael Clarke (91), Simon Katich (67) and Damien Martyn (65) forming the backbone of their effort. Facing a target of 420 runs, England didn't even come close. They started off well enough, putting on 80 for the first wicket, but then it became a procession back to the pavilion. Pietersen again tried to keep the innings together, with 64 not out, but with Vaughan and Bell out for single figures and their last four batsmen all going for ducks, the home side were all out for 180.

McGrath with 4/29 was again the chief destroyer, and Warne claimed 4/64. Sadly, with one wicket short, Warne finished without a place on the Lord's honours board, a rare accolade that has eluded him (a bowler has to take five wickets in an innings to get on the board). At some stage on the day, heavy rain – which raised a big cheer from the English fans! – chased us back to the stand for four hours, but after that the Aussies finished off the job in just over 10 overs. And so the series started off on the wrong foot for England, suffering a crushing 239-run defeat with more than a day to spare.

But now to the 'greatest Test of all time'.

On the morning of the match at Edgbaston, Australia received a huge blow when their bowling hero of Lord's, Glenn McGrath, damaged his ankle when he stepped on a stray ball during a warm-up game of tag rugby. He was out of the match, which must have been quite a boost to the English players. There was no way that Australia could have replaced McGrath with someone of his striking ability.

It also counted in England's favour when Ponting won the toss and asked England to bat. According to the experts, it was a bat-first kind of pitch. As if buoyed by the decision, Strauss and Trescothick played positively and put together 112 for the first wicket before Strauss went for 48. But Trescothick struck a fine 90, and just to show he wouldn't retreat into his shell, he hit Brett Lee for 18 runs in the over just before lunch.

Pietersen was among the runs again for the third time in succession, with 71. He's such a confident, cocky bloke – some would call him arrogant – but his attitude pays off and as long as he gets the runs, no one in England minds. Freddie Flintoff made up for his first-Test failures with 68, entertaining the crowd with some spectacular shots. At the end of the day, England had reached 407 all out – only the second time since World War II that an England team had managed 400 on the first day. So this was something quite special.

Australia had an early setback when Hayden went for a duck, but good scores by Langer, Ponting and Gilchrist, who would eventually be stranded on 49 not out, took them to 309. Spinner Ashley Giles bowled well, taking 3/78, which included the all-important wickets of Ponting and Clarke. Flintoff with 3/52 removed Katich and finished off the tail. England now had a decent lead of 99, and the match was theirs to lose.

Then England had a big scare when Brett Lee seemingly changed the course of the match with a great spell of three wickets in just nine deliveries. Lee eventually took four wickets, but he became expensive after his initial breakthrough, going for more than four runs to the over. And Warne spun his way through the England batting for outstanding figures of 6/46 in 23 overs. Big Freddie Flintoff summarily decided that attack was the best approach and smashed the Aussie bowlers around the park, hitting six fours and four sixes in his 73; one of his sixes off Lee ended up on the pavilion roof.

Despite Flintoff's performance, England discovered just how important their 99-run lead was when Australia sent them all back to the pavilion for only 182.

Australia set about their target of 282 runs looking confident, and Langer and Hayden put together a decent opening partnership of 47. But then Flintoff struck again, this time with the ball, when he dismissed Langer for 28 and Ponting for a duck. Hayden went when the score was on 82, Martyn on 107, Katich on 134, Gilchrist on 136 and Gillespie on 137. England skipper Michael Vaughan claimed the extra half hour to see if they could wrap it up that same day, and they did manage to get the wicket of Michael Clarke just before the close, leaving Australia reeling on 175/8.

All that remained for England to do was to wrap up the last two wickets the next morning. I guess we were all ready for a quick finish. With the Aussies still 102 runs behind, and with only two wickets left, it was all over bar the shouting, as they say. But Shane Warne chose that moment to show what a fine all-rounder he is, and Lee proved that he's no mug with the bat. Slowly but surely they whittled away at the remaining runs. England's supporters grew restless, while the England fielders were becoming very nervous and tense. This was not what they had expected. But then, with the score on 220, Warne, facing Flintoff's bowling, trod on his wicket and a huge cheer went up. Surely this was the end?

Last man Michael Kasprowicz joined Lee and soon also started frustrating the England bowlers, helping Lee at the other end to reduce the target little by little. The tension grew with each over. Fifteen runs short of the target, Kasprowicz cut Flintoff down to third man, where Simon Jones just had to take the catch to end the game. But lo and behold, he spilt it! A huge collective groan rippled through the crowd. Was that the game for England?

The two batsmen kept on chipping away at the target, and finally it was reduced to single figures. It was now anybody's game. With four needed to win, Lee got a single off Harmison's first ball – only three runs between victory and defeat. Kasprowicz faced. He survived the next ball, but the tall Harmison's next delivery reared off the pitch on the leg side. Sadly for Kasprowicz and Australia, it brushed Kasprowicz's glove and wicketkeeper Geraint Jones easily took the leg-side catch.

So near and yet so far! The crowd were beside themselves, as you can imagine. It was a game that could have gone either way, and I tell you, few teams have been so relieved at the end of an innings as England that day!

When England went to Manchester for the third Test, it was with the belief that this Australian side can be beaten. Shane Warne's spin bowling was perceived as the major threat, for it was here, at Old Trafford in 1993, that he produced what the press labelled 'the ball of the century' to bowl out Mike Gatting. England's win at Edgbaston nevertheless ensured that everyone in the country was now talking cricket. They were all behind their men; what more can a team ask for?

Michael Vaughan reacted well to the pressurised situation, scoring 166 in England's first-innings total of 444. Warne not only got his 600th Test wicket, but also scored 90 in Australia's first-innings total of 302. In their second outing, England opener Strauss batted well for his century and Vaughan could declare, leaving Australia a target of 423. Ponting was the mainstay of his team's batting, scoring a century and only departing with the score on 354/9. But Australia was nevertheless in trouble. Lee and McGrath then managed to survive the last four overs for the game to end in a draw. The way the Aussies celebrated, one would have thought they had won the match!

The Aussies and English resumed their rivalry at Trent Bridge, Nottingham, with England batting first and scoring 477, Flintoff leading the way with a well-struck 102 and Geraint Jones with 85. Replying with only 218, the Aussies had to follow on – how often does that happen? This time the batsmen managed a few decent scores to reach 387, but England's target was only 129. The Aussies, and especially Warne with 4/31, made them sweat for it, though, the England wickets falling regularly. On 116/7 it looked a close thing, and in the end England made it with three wickets to spare, going 2-1 up in the series.

I was back as on-field umpire for the fifth Test at The Oval. Australia could now only level the series, but that was all they needed to retain the Ashes. The Test produced great cricket and, lucky me, I had the best seat in the house. Unfortunately, the weather also played a role.

Michael Vaughan won the toss and decided to bat, which proved a good decision. England notched up 373, with Strauss scoring a century and Flintoff again in swashbuckling form with 72. During that innings I could watch the great Shane Warne bowling 37 overs from my end and taking 6/122. Yes, he's a master if ever there was one, and he keeps you, the umpire, on your toes too. He will try anything to get a decision!

Australia came very close to England's score with 367, but when Langer (105) and Hayden (138) put together an opening stand of 185, it looked as if it was going to be a lot more. Even at 323/4 they looked set for a score well beyond 400. But Flintoff bowled a fine 34 overs to claim 5/78 – outstanding figures indeed. We called off play on the second day after tea because of rain and bad light when Australia were 112 without loss, and overnight rain caused play to start 30 minutes late on the third day. Towards the end of the day we again called off play earlier because of bad light. By lunch on the fourth day Australia had reached 356/5, but then lost wickets cheaply and were eventually all out for 367.

Batting again, England were on 7/1 at tea, but we had to stop play because of bad light around 3.45, when the game was still on a knife-edge. The batsmen gladly accepted our light offer and were off in a hurry, and at 6.15 we finally had to abandon play. The decision was not popular with the Australian supporters, and we, the umpires, were in for some criticism, but I will deal with that a bit later.

The next day England struggled, and they were 126/5, then 186/6 and 199/7, just to get Australia excited. But Kevin Pietersen played probably the innings of his life that day, having taken the score to 308/8 by the time he departed with 158 behind his name. I remember how, just before lunch, Brett Lee was hitting him all over the body so that even I felt sorry for him. But after the lunch break Pietersen started attacking the bowlers, and it was right then that I thought to myself: 'This is the best place in the world to be!'

I suspect that Billy Bowden and I gave Pietersen a life about halfway through his innings when he tried to sweep Warne, the ball appearing to go straight onto his boot, from where it was caught by one of the Australian fielders. But I wasn't sure whether the ball had hit ground or boot, and consulted Billy at square leg. Billy insisted that the ball had hit the ground rather than the boot, so we didn't refer the matter upstairs. I later read that Pietersen had thought he was genuinely out, but there you go.

I have to add that Pietersen was dropped three times on the way to his century, and it must have been one of the worst fielding performances I'd ever seen from the Australians. I was at the bowler's end when they dropped Pietersen the first time, and as I walked to square leg after the over, an incident at the 1999 World Cup replayed itself in my mind. I recalled Steve Waugh telling Herschelle Gibbs, when he had accidentally spilt a ball caught off Waugh, 'You've just dropped the World Cup.' I couldn't help thinking, '*They've* just dropped the Ashes.'

All out on 335, England left Australia a target of 342 – but the day was gone. Australia only had time to get to 4/0 in reply. We went off for bad light, but according to the laws we couldn't call off play for another half-hour or so. Common sense, however, said that there was no point in carrying on. When Billy and I went out again, the spectators probably thought we were going to inspect the light, but I said to Billy, 'Let's give them a little surprise. I will go and take off the bails to show that the game is over.' So I walked towards the stumps, flicked off the bails and uprooted a stump to signal the end of the Test. Oh, boy, did that gesture set off an English celebration!

As mentioned earlier, our decision to offer the light to the England batsmen on the fourth day drew some criticism. I firmly believe that our decision was the correct one. For a start, the reading on the light meter was identical to the reading when we offered the light to Australia on Day 2. Even though two spin bowlers were operating, batting conditions were not good, and it was unfair to the batsmen to let play continue. When the fast bowlers are bowling, there is a very specific level of light that is acceptable. As soon as it dips below that level, you offer the light to the batsmen. We give the spin bowlers a bit more leeway, but once we think the scale has tipped against the batsmen, we offer the light. The fact is that in bad light a batsman can still lose sight of the ball in the air, even if it was bowled slowly.

Geoff Boycott criticised our decision, but it's ironic that, in 1977, when he played for England in the Ashes, he chose to leave the field when he was offered the light and Australia had a spinner on. However, in contrast, former Australia wicketkeeper Rod Marsh agreed with our decision. He told the BBC: 'You can't play Test cricket in this light – I don't care what anyone says. It's unfair to the batsmen, even if the spinners are bowling.'

But all the ifs and buts meant nothing in the end. England was ecstatic for having won the Ashes. It wouldn't be long before they had to go and defend it, though – in Australia.

7

From Ashes to Ashes

" *When I stood in the Ashes again, in 2009, it marked a very special milestone for me – standing in my 100th Test in the second Test of the series at Lord's. My achievement was announced over the public address system before the start of play, and it was an incredible moment for me when I actually walked out onto the hallowed Lord's turf.* **"**

In December 2006 I had another stint in the Ashes, contested in Australia. I was appointed to officiate in the second Test in Adelaide, the third Test in Perth and the fourth Test in Melbourne. The first match would be handled by Steve Bucknor and Billy Bowden. As could be expected, there was a lot of media hype leading up to the series. The Aussies, it was reported, wanted to take revenge for 2005 and win back the Ashes. I was looking forward to the battle as much as the cricketing public. It was only my second time standing in the Ashes in Australia, the first having been in 2002.

Australia could not have asked for a better start to the series. In their first innings, they knocked up a huge score of 602/9, thereby ensuring that they couldn't lose the match. Ponting played a real captain's innings, scoring 196. England came in but folded to 157 all out, Ian Bell top-scoring with 50. In their second innings,

Ponting declared on 202/1, with Langer on 100 not out and Ponting himself on 60 not out. In England's second innings, Collingwood (96) and Pietersen (92) tried bravely, but they were still 277 runs short when their innings ended.

When Steve Bucknor and I stepped out onto the Adelaide turf for the start of the second Test, we became the most experienced umpiring pair ever to stand together in a Test, sharing 191 Tests between us. Steve had 114 matches behind his name; I had 77. Our record was broken two years later when Darrell Hair (77) and Steve Bucknor (then on 123) teamed up in the England vs New Zealand Test at Old Trafford for a shared total of exactly 200 Tests. It turned out to be Hair's last Test outing.

But back to Adelaide ... England went in to bat first on a slow pitch that was disheartening to the bowlers. Even Warne struggled to get some turn. Bell and Collingwood dug in, until Bell went for 60. Collingwood reached his hundred early on the second day and Pietersen got his ton before lunch later in the day. Collingwood went past 150, and carried on to 200. When he reached this milestone, he became the first England player to score a double century in Australia since Wally Hammond 70 years before. He was out soon after for 206, by which time he and Pietersen had put together a partnership of 310, a fourth-wicket record for England against Australia. Pietersen, playing in his 20th Test match, went for 158 for the third time. England's new skipper, Andrew Flintoff, declared on 551/6.

Australia were not to be outdone, and Ponting, dropped on 35, made his 10th hundred, finishing on 142, and Michael Clarke, who only played because Shane Watson was injured, made 124 as Australia scored 513 all out. Matthew Hoggard managed the remarkable figures of 7/109 on the slow pitch.

England started their second innings with little prospect of anything dramatic happening on the final day, especially when they were 69/1. But then the England wickets kept tumbling, and I think there were about three fours in four hours before they succumbed to 129 all out. It was Shane Warne who had once again raised hopes of a possible victory for Australia. He got the important wickets of Strauss, Pietersen, Flintoff and Giles, and took 4/49 in 32 overs, of which no fewer than 12 were maidens. The ball with which he got Pietersen was a real beauty, bowled around his legs and hitting the outside of off-stump!

Set a target of 168 in 36 overs, Australia had a bit of a hiccup when Ponting and Martyn were out soon after each other, but it was the dependable Mike Hussey with 61 who saw them home with 19 balls to spare.

England, of course, had to win at the WACA (Western Australian Cricket Association ground) in Perth to stay in contention for the Ashes, and when Australia reached a mediocre 244 in their first innings, their hopes were high. Steve Harmison had a good bowling spell, taking 4/48, and Monty Panesar spun the ball well for fine figures of 5/92, which was probably an omen that Shane Warne could be doing well later. But the England batsmen, apart from Pietersen with 70, undid all their bowlers' good work, collapsing to 215 all out. At 8/155, when Hoggard went, and again on 175/9, when Pietersen walked, they didn't look like they would get to 200, but by the time Harmison was last man out, they had managed to take the score to 215.

Australia then took control of the match, Hayden scoring 92, Hussey 103, and Clarke and Gilchrist each finishing on an unbeaten century to allow Ponting to declare at 527 for five. Gilchrist was at his devastating best, scoring his 102 off just 59 balls, a strike rate of 172 – and this was supposed to be Test cricket! This left England the massive second-innings target of 557 runs.

Their effort started off disastrously, with Strauss going for a duck, but Bell (87) batted well and the second wicket only went at 172. Opener Alistair Cook stuck around for almost seven hours for 116, but thereafter the only man to make a significant score in the context of the target set was Pietersen, who was stranded on an unbeaten 60 when England fell to 350 all out. Like Panesar, Warne spun the ball well and finished with 115/4 off almost 40 overs.

So in the end Australia won by 206 runs to go 3-0 up in the series and regained the Ashes. The beer was flowing freely all around Australia. From the first Test, the Aussies had looked determined to take the series; England, although fielding just about the same players as in 2005, was a different bunch from the previous Ashes.

After the Test, Warne announced that he was going to call it a day after the close of the series, and by the time the fifth Test arrived, Glenn McGrath and Justin Langer had announced their intentions to do likewise. So, standing in my last Test in the series as on-field umpire in Melbourne, I was going to be part of a great occasion: Shane Warne would retire from international cricket by saying farewell to his home crowd at the MCG. And, typically the man for the big moment, he made his exit in Melbourne in grand style.

At the time, Warne's total for Test wickets stood on 699, the highest for any bowler in the world. The whole of the MCG crowd were going to sit on the edge of their seats, waiting for that big moment in history when he reached 700, the first bowler to reach this milestone. The first day started off on a miserably cold and damp note, and a steady morning drizzle delayed play by half an hour. Finally, in the 41st over of the day, when two England wickets had already fallen, hometown boy Warnie was introduced. He needed only four overs to claim his 700th scalp.

Andrew Strauss was on 50 when Warne flighted a ball that dipped into the rough, spun past Strauss's loose cover drive and crashed into the middle stump. The whole ground erupted and, boy, did Warne celebrate! 'I was going to keep on running, but I got puffed!' he joked afterwards.

England was disappointing once again, succumbing for just 159. Warne delivered one of his best performances to please his home crowd and took 5/39 in just over 17 magic overs. It was also the 37th time in his 144 Tests that he had taken five wickets in an innings. What a great bowler this man was! He had great accuracy for most of his spells, and he could spin the ball prodigiously – the kind of bowler you would rather not bat against.

Australia had a shaky start and teetered on 84/5; top batsmen Ponting, Hussey, Clarke and Gilchrist scored just 19 runs between them. But then Hayden and Andrew Symonds took the game by the scruff of the neck, and it was only with the score at 363 that Hayden went for 153.

I turned down quite a few lbw appeals, and according to the press Hayden was lucky to have survived two of those from Hoggard, but I thought otherwise. At one stage Hoggard was staring incredulously into my eyes after making a strong appeal against Matthew Hayden. Warne gave his home crowd further reason to cheer when he hit an unbeaten 40, knocking 11 runs in one over and nine in another, both off Sajid Mahmood.

When Symonds lost his wicket for 156, the score had gone to 383/8, and Australia was eventually all out for 419.

In their second innings, England had to score 260 just to make the Aussies bat again, but they fell well short: all out for 161. This time Lee was the main destroyer, with 4/47.

Warne was bowling from my side of the pitch, and typical Warnie, he put as much pressure on me as he possibly could, emitting a gasp of incredulity now and then when I didn't give the batsman out. Had he been allowed to umpire his own bowling, England wouldn't have got to 50!

Australia won the match by an innings and 99 runs with two whole days to spare, going 4-0 up in the series. Warne received the Man of the Match award, which must have pleased the crowd and the man himself. The final day, which was really only the third day, fell on Boxing Day, and everyone had expected the world record attendance of 90 800 in 1960/61 to be bettered (Australia had played the West Indies), but the numbers fell short on 89 155. It was still a new record for the Ashes, though. Looking back now, there were a lot of memorable moments for me during the three Ashes Tests in which I'd officiated.

Australia went on to take the fifth Test in Sydney as well, winning by 10 wickets. With England scoring 291 in their first innings and Australia replying with 393, England were required to knock up a few hundred to make a game of it. But for the umpteenth time they failed, all out for a mere 147, and the Aussies knocked off the required target with all wickets intact.

The victory was Australia's 12th consecutive win and their 16th out of 17 (with one draw) since the 2005 Ashes. They also became the first Australian side since the team of 1920/21 to achieve an Ashes whitewash.

When I stood in the Ashes again, in 2009, it marked a very special milestone for me – standing in my 100th Test in the second Test of the series at Lord's. My achievement was announced over the public address system before the start of play, and it was an incredible moment for me when I actually walked out onto the hallowed Lord's turf. I remember Ricky Ponting running over to shake my hand, and then each of the players came to congratulate me.

One hundred Tests. I could hardly believe it. I had become only the second umpire in the history of cricket (after Steve Bucknor) to stand in a century of Tests. What made it extra special was that only five days earlier I had become the first umpire ever to officiate in 200 One Day Internationals, giving me an unprecedented double.

I couldn't help thinking back to the day that it had all started, way back on Boxing Day 1992 in the third Test between South Africa and India at St George's Park. It seemed so long ago. There I was, this greenhorn Test umpire, all nerves, but very excited. Did I think of 100 Tests then? Never in your life!

The first Ashes Test in Cardiff was drawn, and to be honest, the Aussies were a bit unlucky not to have pulled that one off. England scored 435 in their first innings, and Australia replied with a massive 674/6 declared. Ponting, Marcus North, Katich and Haddin all scored centuries, but play ended with England on 252/9.

Strangely, at that stage England had not won at Lord's since 1934. So the big question was: Would they be able to end that drought? I was standing with Billy Doctrove – nicknamed 'Denzel Washington' by some – when England went out to bat first. They started very positively. Strauss scored 161 and Alastair Cook 95 in their first-innings total of 425. The second day was interrupted by rain, and for the first time in a Lord's Test match the flood-lights were switched on. But the gloom carried over into the Australians' first innings. At 156/8 at the end of Day 2, they were still trailing England by 269 runs. James Anderson, with 4/36, bowled with pace and got good movement to rip through the Australian batting. Resilient tail-end batting eventually pushed them to 215 all out.

England then replied with 311/6 declared, Matthew Prior scoring 61 and Collingwood 54. This left the Aussies with a huge fourth-innings target of 522.

England had looked like wrapping up the game on the Sunday, once quick Australian wickets had followed the overnight declaration, but spirited resistance by Clarke, with 125 not out, and Haddin, with 80 not out, took their score of 128/5 to 313/5 by the close. The Australian innings was, however, marked by controversial umpiring decisions, and Billy Doctrove and I were not the most popular guys back in Australia that night.

On that fourth day, Simon Katich was caught in the gully to a ball from Flintoff. On the replay it looked to be a no-ball, which I hadn't picked up. But the bigger controversy involved the dis-missal of Phillip Hughes to a claimed catch by Strauss. Hughes edged Flintoff low to first slip, where Strauss appeared to take the catch. Hughes wanted to walk, but from the non-striker's end Ponting told him to wait for the decision.

I consulted Billy Doctrove at square leg, who confirmed the

ball had carried, so we didn't deem it necessary to refer the catch to the third umpire, Nigel Long, and I sent Hughes on his way. Replays afterwards were inconclusive on whether Strauss had caught the ball cleanly. Just the previous day we had referred a similar incident to the third umpire when Ravi Bopara was batting, which resulted in a benefit-of-the-doubt ruling. Not surprisingly, we were accused of inconsistency and double standards.

Hussey's dismissal was also controversial; he pushed forward to Graeme Swann in Swann's second over, and the ball snicked into the hands of Collingwood at slip. England appealed instantly and Doctrove didn't hesitate to give Hussey out. But replays suggested the deviation had been entirely off the pitch and not off the bat.

On the last day, Andrew Flintoff brought an end to Australia's 75-year unbeaten run at Lord's. Having taken five wickets in the innings, and having already scored a century at Lord's, he became only the sixth cricketer to put his name on both honours boards at the ground. He only needed four balls to remove Haddin, with his overnight score still on 80, caught at second slip.

Mitchell Johnson kept Australian hopes alive, timing the ball sweetly with nine fours in his 63. But when Swann yorked Clarke, the writing was on the wall, and England won by 115 runs.

After the game, match referee Jeff Crowe said that although there had been some confusion as to why one catching incident was referred and not the other, it was simply a question of whether the on-field umpire was able to make the call himself or needed input from the third umpire. If the umpire was confident of his decision, he would make the call himself, regardless of how near or far away from him the incident had taken place.

Later that year, in October, a more detailed review process was put in place. Interestingly, Strauss wasn't sure it would be completely helpful. 'I don't know what the solution is, to be honest with you,' he said in an interview. 'I still maintain that I caught that ball. It's tricky because it looks like it hasn't carried, but I still firmly believe that it did.'

In Birmingham, the wet English weather delayed the start of the third Test, and Aleem Dar and I went out twice to inspect the field. It was soaked, and with no end to the rain in sight, chances of any play looked slim. Of course this wasn't helping Australia's cause. Their game plan also required an instant rethink when Haddin suffered a suspected broken finger in the warm-up and had to be replaced with Graham Manou.

Ironically, it was four years earlier, when I was also standing in the Ashes in Birmingham, that Australia suffered a similar blow when Glenn McGrath hurt his ankle on the morning of the game. The England side, however, also suffered a big setback when the injured Pietersen had to be replaced by Ian Bell.

But play eventually did start, and by close of play Australia had raced to 126/1, with Shane Watson on 62 not out. But he was out on the same score the next day, and as none of the other Australian batsmen could rattle up a big tally, they were all out for 263. Anderson was among the wickets again, taking 5/80, and was well supported by Graham Onions with 4/58. Onions stood on a hat-trick when he'd first dismissed Watson and next ball angled a delivery into Hussey, who shouldered arms and then watched helplessly as the ball slammed into the top of off-stump. But then Onions's would-be hat-trick ball to Michael Clarke was pitched short on the leg side.

England replied with a solid 376 all out, with Strauss (69), Flintoff (74) and Broad (55) all contributing decent scores. Unfortunately for Australia, with England's score on 116/2 on the second day, bad light and rain stopped play for the day, and on the third day we had no play at all. Aleem Dar and I were particularly concerned about the soggy run-ups and the damp outfield, and we called Ponting and Strauss onto the field during two inspections. We eventually agreed that the conditions were suitable for play, but by then no fewer than five sessions had been lost. So the England innings resumed only on the fourth day, when they took their score to 376.

Australia's frustration with the delays and the match situation in general came to a boil during one of Mitchell Johnson's overs in which he conceded 15 runs, with Swann and Stuart Broad at the crease, and it provided some added entertainment to the vociferous Edgbaston crowd. Swann had slashed a four over the slips, which really cheesed off Johnson, who followed it up with a no-ball bouncer – as well as a barrage of choice invective.

Swann had a few things of his own to say, and Broad, at the non-striker's end, joined in the verbal fray. Swann then steered Johnson for four through backward point, which left him fuming. The bowler won his personal duel with Swann when he had him caught at cover, but Broad kept his fury alive with a back-foot whack for four. The upshot was Johnson and Broad nose to nose at the non-striker's end.

At the close Australia had 88/2, still trailing on England's first-innings score, and the chances of them winning looked remote. With no result in sight, Australia decided to declare on 375/5 on the final day. Watson and Hussey both scored 50s, Marcus North fell four runs short of his century and Clarke was 103 not out on the declaration.

I remember Clarke having had two moments of good fortune to progress to his 100. On 92 he had his off-stump clipped as he played inside a delivery from Broad, but lo and behold, the bail remained in place! Four runs later he slashed at Bopara and was caught by Anderson at wide slip – but to his great relief I signalled a no-ball. Poor North, however, was denied his hundred by a stunning catch by Anderson as he drove uppishly and Anderson, fielding at gully, took off to his right and just clung on with his right hand.

And so my umpiring in the 2009 Ashes came to an end.

Australia kept their Ashes hopes alive in the fourth Test at Headingley in Leeds when they beat England by an innings and 80 runs. Scoring 445 in their first innings, they skittled England for a mere 102, and sent them all back to the pavilion for 263 in their second innings. Johnson (5/69) and Siddle (5/21) were Australia's best bowlers, but Broad himself had a fine return of 6/91 in the Australian innings.

So everything would come down to the fifth Test at The Oval. England set a solid first-innings total of 332, with Bell top-scoring with 72, and assumed control of the match when they bundled out Australia for 160. They then drove their advantage home by scoring 373/9 in their second innings. The newcomer to the side, South African–born Jonathan Trott, top-scored with 119. The target was just too much for Australia, and despite a fighting 121 by Hussey, they finished almost 200 runs short. And the Ashes went back to England again.

At the time a lot of criticism was aimed at the umpires in the series – when is it not? – for some of the decisions, especially from Australian quarters. According to them, some of our decisions had 'undermined' (as one hack put it) Australia's chances in the Ashes, and they didn't get the rub of the green. Shane Warne, for example, was especially unhappy about me not giving out Ian Bell lbw to Johnson in England's first innings at Edgbaston.

I certainly had no problem with the umpire review system that was introduced a few months later, in October 2009. More and more cricket umpires trust each other and work together as a team, and players are generally understanding of our efforts to get our decisions right. They realise that making the right call is our primary goal. And if that means we occasionally have to go back and change a decision we've made with the help of replays, then I, for one, am prepared to do that.

8

A double century in ODIs

" Halfway through the 2007 World Cup tournament I started thinking that I had had enough of it. I had arrived in the West Indies two weeks before the start of the tournament, and by then I was fed up and just wanted to go home. Surely four weeks should be long enough to complete the World Cup? "

Cricket traditionalists sometimes have a lot to say about the nature and spirit of the One Day International, but it has always been a welcome change from the Test scene for players and umpires alike. To some, the advent of Twenty20, or T20, in turn, has been a welcome change to the 50-overs ODI. Cricket is supposed to entertain, and judging by crowd attendances, ODIs – and, lately, Twenty20 especially, are doing the job just fine. And I don't think I'm mistaken when I say that the shorter formats help to sharpen a batsman's reflexes and hone his aggressive stroke play.

For us as umpires it brings welcome relief from the monotony of drawn-out five-day Tests, but having said that, to me Test cricket will always be number one on the cricket calendar and the benchmark for any professional cricketer. But there is also no doubt that the pace of the ODI has rubbed off on the Test, and where in the good old days teams were happy to crawl along at two runs an over, that is no longer the case, unless one is fighting for survival.

I have stood in quite a few ODIs in my time – more than any other international umpire, in fact. I overtook David Shepherd's record of 172 ODI appearances in April 2007, and today I have more than 200 matches behind my name. Since my first international ODI in Port Elizabeth in 1992 (South Africa vs India), I have stood in matches in all parts of the world, but mostly in South Africa, of course, and in Australia and the West Indies. You can imagine how much cricket I watched during that time and that some magic moments are still engrained in my memory, but that the lesser ones have faded over the years.

On Saturday 11 July 2009, I reached the 200th ODI milestone when I stood in the second ODI between Ireland and Kenya in Dublin. It was a highly emotional moment for me when, to mark the occasion, I received a special trophy from Cricket Ireland president Arthur Vince on behalf of the International Cricket Council.

Soon afterwards I also became the second umpire to achieve the double of 100 ODIs and 100 Tests when I stood in the second Ashes Test at Lord's. I could look back upon my career with a lot of satisfaction; it has been a very rewarding journey, indeed. During my ODI career, I have had the privilege of standing in the ICC World Championships in 2002, 2004 and 2006. In 2004 and 2006 I also had the additional honour of standing as on-field umpire in the final of both of these tournaments. I was also privileged to officiate in the World Cups of 1999, 2003 and 2007, but the one milestone that has eluded me so far is to stand in a World Cup final. I've stood in semi-finals of the World Cup, but the closest I got to a final was as third umpire in the 2007 final in the West Indies.

The ICC Champions Trophy is perhaps not as glamorous a tournament as the World Cup, but it is nevertheless a competition that the fans, players and umpires enjoy equally, if not more sometimes. Like the World Cup, it's the type of occasion where anything can happen to any team on the day, and many a favourite has unexpectedly dropped out in the past. I can immediately think of the 2009 event in South Africa, where the hosts ended up stone last in their pool – against all expectations. What a disappointment for the home fans!

I had my first opportunity in the championships in 2002, when it was held in Sri Lanka. I stood in three of the pool matches, all involving two of the minor teams, Zimbabwe (vs India and then England) and the Netherlands (vs Pakistan), and all three were played in Colombo. Two years later, at the 2004 championship in England, I had a much bigger role to play, standing in one of the semi-finals and then the final.

In the semi-final at Edgbaston in Birmingham the hosts played attractive cricket and easily beat Australia, winning by six wickets and 21 balls to spare. Not that they had an easy target. The Aussies knocked up 259/9, Damien Martyn scoring 65 and Michael Clarke 42. England was not overawed at the required run rate of more than 5.5 an over and raced to the target with only four wickets down, Trescothick (81), Vaughan (86) and Strauss (52 not out) leading their effort.

I was then appointed to officiate in the final at The Oval, where England faced the West Indies. Trescothick was going great guns on 104 when he was run out, and considering his century, England should have done better than their 217 all out. They had set an easy enough target for the Windies, especially with the likes of Gayle, Sarwan, Lara and Chanderpaul in the team, but things became quite close. Even though the Windies had seven balls remaining at the end, they had only two wickets standing. It was an agonising time for the Windies fans when, on 147/8, their team looked dead and buried, but a ninth-wicket partnership saw them through, Chanderpaul top-scoring with 47.

India hosted the next ICC Champions Trophy, in 2006, but the final at the Brabourne Stadium, Mumbai, between Australia and the West Indies – playing in their second consecutive Champions Trophy final – was an anticlimax for the fans and a disappointing conclusion to the tournament. Earlier on, Australia had eliminated New Zealand at the Punjab Cricket Association Stadium, Mohali, to advance to the final, and the West Indies beat South Africa.

In the final itself, the West Indies batted first and were all out for 138 in just over 30 overs. When rain interrupted play, Australia's target was further reduced to 117 in 35 overs according to the Duckworth-Lewis method, and the result became a mere formality. Guided by Shane Watson (57 not out), the Aussies reached their goal with just two wickets down and 41 balls to spare, even though Gilchrist went cheaply.

I did not stand in the 2009 championships in South Africa, but, for the record, Australia beat England by nine wickets with 49 balls remaining at Centurion in the one semi-final, and that after the England batsmen had put a decent total of 259 on the board. Shane Watson (136 not out) and Ricky Ponting (111 not out) were the stars of the match. In the final, also at Centurion, the Aussies also easily accounted for New Zealand, winning by six wickets and still 28 balls to spare.

Apart from the ICC championships and the World Cup, I have officiated in numerous other ODI series since 1992, but because there were so many, I will only be able to highlight those matches and player performances that have stood out most for me.

I have already referred to my very first international one-dayer way back in 1992 in Port Elizabeth, and because it was my first, I remember it like yesterday. It wasn't a great match from a spectator's point of view, India being dismissed for 147 in the 50th over and the Proteas easily reaching the target with six wickets standing and a few overs remaining. I also stood in the next ODI of the series in Bloemfontein, and in East London, but the former will mostly be remembered for the spectators who invaded the pitch after Kepler Wessels reached 50, and again when Andrew Hudson reached 50 and, later, 100. The Proteas dominated the series, winning five of the seven matches.

The West Indies and Pakistan visited the Republic late in 1993 for the Total International Series, and I stood in two of the ODIs, in Cape Town and Centurion. The match in Cape Town was a low-scoring affair, though exciting, with the local side scraping home. They had set a meagre target of 141, but the inconsistent Windies fell four runs short. Hansie Cronjé and Meyrick Pringle each took 3/27 to constrict the West Indian innings.

In Centurion, Pakistan set the Proteas a mediocre target of 220, which should not have been difficult for the South African batting line-up to achieve. They could, however, only manage 198/9, and it is seldom that I have seen cricket suicide being committed as in Pretoria that day. First Hansie, then Daryll Cullinan, and finally Dave Richardson all had to trudge back to the pavilion after being run out.

When Australia toured South Africa in early 1994, I umpired in three of the ODIs, and each had its exciting moments. In my hometown, Port Elizabeth, the Australians bounced back from defeats in the first two matches with an 88-run victory, knocking up 281/9, with David Boon (76) passing 5 000 one-day runs and Dean Jones (67) going beyond the 6 000 mark. It was Allan Border, however, who provided the real fireworks, smashing 40 from just 17 balls. Poor Fanie de Villiers had to watch how 19 runs came off one of his overs. The Proteas were bowled out for 193, and it was Shane Warne who'd made the biggest inroads, with 4/36.

At Buffalo Park in East London, Mark and Steve Waugh put up an unbroken partnership of 88 in Australia's seven-wicket win after South Africa were bowled out for a mere 158. Steve Waugh was by far the dominant batsman, hitting 67 off 60 balls.

In the seventh ODI at Newlands, Australia won by 36 runs, Mark Taylor and Mark Waugh sharing a very good partnership of 123 in their total of 242 to set up victory. South Africa faced some extremely tight bowling and never really looked like scoring the required runs. Again it was Shane Warne, this time with 3/31 off 10 overs, who really strangled the middle part of the South African innings.

I stood in three of the matches when England played the Proteas in early 1996, including the last one in Port Elizabeth. President Nelson Mandela was there to watch Hansie's boys wrap up the seven-match series with a convincing 54-run victory to take the series 6-1, and also to hand over the trophy to Hansie. Outstanding bowling by Darren Gough, with 4/33 – including two wickets with consecutive balls – restricted the Proteas to 218/9. But the South African bowlers came right back to skittle England for 154, and it was the veteran Fanie de Villiers who was the main man with 4/32.

At the beginning of 1997 I stood in the Standard Bank Series between South Africa, India and Zimbabwe, which South Africa won. The first final in Durban was washed out, but the local side made sure to capture the title in the second final, also in Durban.

But one of the more remarkable matches in which I stood during the tournament was a day-night fixture between India and Zimbabwe in Paarl. Chasing Zim's 236, India was in trouble at 110/5, but then Robin Singh kept them in the hunt until they needed two to win off the last ball. Ebbo Brandes bowled the final ball wide of leg stump, and as the batsmen ran a bye, the keeper aimed the ball at the near wicket but missed; Brandes pounced on it and threw down the wicket at the other end to run out Robin Singh right under my nose. I gave Singh out, but at the same time I had to signal a wide. To their dismay, the Zimbabweans had to discover that they had only tied …

Until April 1997 I stood in ODIs in my home country only, but once I became a full-time ICC umpire, I started umpiring overseas in ODIs as well. My first outing was in Toronto, of all places, which you would associate with ice hockey rather than with cricket. India was playing Pakistan, and I stood on-field in four matches and sat upstairs as TV umpire in two more.

In September 1999 I was off to Singapore, which is not really associated with the game either, to officiate in the Coca-Cola

Challenge between India and the West Indies. The event has special memories for me because of the fact that it was the first – and last – time I was approached by a bloke in the match-fixing Mafia. I cover that episode in the chapter on match fixing.

The West Indies won the final of the series by four wickets and with 14 balls to spare, following a splendid 124 by Ricardo Powell in chasing a stiff target of 255. Tendulkar disappointed, going for a duck in the first over of India's innings, but Dravid kept things together with an unbeaten 103. Nevertheless, the West Indies won the tournament.

I started the millennium umpiring in the Standard Bank Triangular Tournament, which involved South Africa, England and Zimbabwe, and, predictably, South Africa and England contested the final at the Wanderers. The Proteas won comfortably by 38 runs, in spite of setting a modest target of 150. Andrew Caddick (4/19) and Darren Gough (3/18) must have thought they had won the match for England, but Shaun Pollock showed what a fighter he was with excellent bowling figures of 5/20. England were all back in the pavilion for 111. Polly had a fine tournament and was deservedly named Player of the Series.

Two months later, in April, when the Proteas took on Australia in three matches for the Challenge Series trophy, the unfortunate memories of the previous year's World Cup semi-final were still fresh in the South African players' minds. Lance Klusener, especially, must still have been having nightmares, as he was at the crease, steering the Proteas towards an unlikely victory, when the misunderstanding between him and Allan Donald led to a run-out. The match was drawn and the Aussies went through to the final. All of South Africa was in mourning.

But in April 2000 it was South Africa who came back almost from the dead to take the Challenge Series trophy, and it was none other than Klusener who pulled the lower order together to set up the victory. In a packed and noisy Wanderers stadium (the biggest crowd in its history), Shaun Pollock, playing his 100th match for the Proteas, made a huge impact on Australia's innings, taking 4/37 and restricting their total to 206.

But then it was South Africa's turn to bat, and Brett Lee was as quick as I've ever seen him. He ripped through the Proteas' middle order, bowling the second-fastest delivery in the history of the game at 156 km/h (only 2 km/h slower than Ahktar). South Africa's reputation as 'chokers' was almost confirmed when they slipped from 91/2 to 91/5, and then to 122/6. The crowd went quiet. Fortunately, after a cautious start, Klusener and Boucher then formed an unbroken seventh-wicket partnership of 87 off 96 balls, which wrested the initiative from the Aussies and helped the Proteas to 209/6.

At the end of the match, Aussie skipper Steve Waugh conceded that South Africa had been the better side in the three-match series.

However, when the two teams met again in 2002, it was a different story. In both the Test and one-day series, Australia wiped the floor with South Africa. At the end of the fourth ODI in the series, the Aussies had taken a 4-0 lead, and what a pleasure it was to see Gilchrist hammer another century in Durban, where I stood on-field. (I also umpired a match in Potchefstroom.) Under most circumstances, South Africa's 267/6 might well have been a winning total, but Gillie was going at more than a run a ball, and Australia cruised home with 14 balls to spare. Gillie's innings wasn't flawless, but it was as entertaining as it was brutal. The faster Nantie Hayward tried to bowl, the harder Gilchrist smashed him.

In the last clash, at Newlands, the South Africans finally broke their duck with a 65-run victory, but the series had shown how wide a gap had opened between Australia and the rest of the cricket world.

In December 2002 I stood in three of the VB Triangular Series matches in Australia, contested between the Aussies, England and Sri Lanka, and again the Australians dominated the show. England slumped to a seven-wicket defeat by Australia in the first game in Sydney, and the Aussies then overpowered Sri Lanka by a massive 142 runs at the WACA (after setting a daunting 306-run target).

The following season, in the West Indies, Ponting's boys had clinched the series 4-0 by the time I was standing in the fourth ODI of the seven-match series in Port of Spain, but the West Indies restored some pride in the remaining matches to come back to 3-4. Australia won the fourth ODI by 67 runs, Gilchrist top-scoring with 84 in their innings of 286/5. The West Indies won the fifth and sixth ODIs, in Port of Spain and St George's, beating the Aussies by three wickets in the sixth. Gilchrist was among the runs again with 64 in the Australian total of 252. Wavell Hinds, however, stole the show with a superb, unbeaten 125 runs.

I don't know if the Australians had lost interest by then, with the series already decided, but the West Indies won the last ODI in St George's by nine wickets and with 39 balls remaining. Lehmann top-scored for Australia with 107, and the Windies, chasing 248, reached their target with nine wickets intact. While Hinds scored another century (103 off 130 balls), I enjoyed Brian Lara's innings more – he smashed 75 not out off 65 balls. At the end of the tournament Ricky Ponting said that the series had dragged on for too long – as it had in South Africa in 2002 – and had got a bit monotonous, and suggested that five games would be better than seven.

In 2005, I officiated in the fourth, fifth and sixth ODI in the much-awaited six-match Pakistan/India series. Pakistan won the match in Ahmedabad by three wickets off the last ball to level the series. Although Tendulkar scored 123 runs, it was a bit on the slow side, coming as it did off 192 balls, but he nevertheless helped his side to a big score (315). Pakistan reached that total with seven wickets down, Inzamam-ul-Haq scoring a patient 60 not out.

The most spectacular innings I was privileged to see in the series was a whirlwind 102 by Shahid Afridi – off only 76 balls!

He set Pakistan on their way to a five-wicket victory in the fifth match in Kampur with 47 balls remaining, chasing 250 for a win. What a player to have in your side! With bat in hand he can so easily change the course of a game in just a few overs, and he's a more than useful bowler, too. Every time I saw Afridi after that, whether from behind the stumps or on TV, I would inevitably think back to that day in Kampur when he absolutely destroyed the Indian bowling.

In the sixth ODI in Delhi, Pakistan won the game to take the series 4-2.

Later in 2005 I watched England take on Australia in Leeds, at Lord's and at The Oval, and the hosts started off on an excellent foot in the first game when they beat the Aussies by nine wickets and with 24 balls still remaining, chasing a modest total of 220. But the visitors came back strongly at Lord's, winning the second match by seven wickets with six overs to spare in pursuit of another modest target (224). Ponting played a captain's innings with 111.

At The Oval the runs were again in the 220s, and chasing 229 to win, Australia didn't exactly have to set the ground alight. Even so, Gilchrist's undefeated 121 came off just 101 balls at a strike rate of 120 per cent. It's always a joy to watch this man, as there's never a dull moment. He believes a ball is there to be hit, no matter what the situation. Someone told me that on one occasion Gillie was standing on a duck-pair in a Test when he simply whacked the second ball he received for six! Australia went on to win the match at The Oval by eight wickets and with 91 balls remaining.

I reached a special milestone when, in April 2006, I stood in my 150th ODI in Abu Dhabi, in a match between India and Pakistan. Before then, only Dave Shepherd – who by then had retired – had officiated in that many one-dayers. At that stage I had 73 Tests under my belt, and the thought of achieving the double of 100 Tests and 200 ODIs wasn't all that far-fetched. In

Abu Dhabi, both India and Pakistan won a match each, but it wasn't a great series, and Dravid's 92 was the highest score of the tournament.

In February/March 2008 I was looking forward to the Commonwealth Bank Series in Australia, where the hosts, India and Sri Lanka – three of the world's top one-day sides – were to slog it out. I stood in seven matches, including the first two – Australia vs India at Brisbane and India vs Sri Lanka (also Brisbane) – but because of bad weather, neither match produced a result. I then stood in the fourth ODI – Australia vs India at Melbourne – but the scores were low for both teams. At least the sixth match – Australia vs Sri Lanka at Perth – produced something worthwhile in the form of another century by Gilchrist (118 off 132 balls – much slower than usual!). The hosts won that game by 63 runs.

My next match, the ninth of the series – Australia vs Sri Lanka at Melbourne – was again rain-affected, but at least it produced a result. Australia won by 24 runs on the Duckworth-Lewis method. I also stood in the first of the two finals in Sydney, where India beat Australia by six wickets. This was Tendulkar's match: he hit 117 off 120 balls. India also won the second final in Brisbane, beating Australia by nine runs, to win the tournament.

In 2009, I umpired on-field in three of the Proteas/Australia ODIs in South Africa, and I was also the TV umpire in another two. It was an eagerly awaited series, as South Africa had unexpectedly beaten Australia 4-1 in Australia shortly before. The first match in Durban produced a big win for the visitors, by 141 runs. Mike Hussey played the best innings of the lot, making 83 off 79 balls in Australia's score of 286. The South Africans then reversed the tables at Centurion, winning by seven wickets with 142 balls remaining.

I stood again in the third match at Newlands, where the home side's 289 proved just too much for the Aussies. I was impressed by the young Roelof van der Merwe, who was playing in only his second match for the Proteas. He was not overawed by the occa-sion at all, recording fine bowling figures of 3/37 in his 10 overs and taking the wickets of Clarke and Mike Hussey.

The Proteas easily took the fourth match, winning by 61 runs after scoring 317/6. South Africa's naughty boy Herschelle Gibbs led the way with 110 off 116 balls. Dale Steyn, who had a tremen-dous season, took 4/44 and Van der Merwe 3/46 to make sure the Aussies didn't come close to the target. I finished the series in the fifth ODI at the Wanderers, which the Aussies won by 47 runs, but it was too little, too late for them.

My next series in 2009 would not have excited too many fans – except in Ireland and Kenya – but it meant a personal milestone for me. On Saturday 11 July I umpired in my 200th ODI, standing in the second ODI between Ireland and Kenya in Dublin. As mentioned earlier, I received a special trophy from Cricket Ireland president Arthur Vince on behalf of the ICC.

During the past few years a new craze has taken hold of cricket fans all over the world – the Twenty20, or T20, game. If I may say so, I believe that success in this format of the game has as much to do with luck as with talent, as even a normally average player may get runs or wickets on any day. But it is the kind of game that fans relish in their busy lifestyles and, as in the 50-over game, there is always a result. In addition, it is accompanied by all kinds of entertainment, giving spectators extra value for money.

I have so far umpired in only eight T20 internationals. In the first, South Africa took on Pakistan in Johannesburg on 2 February 2007. I stood in two more – South Africa vs West Indies, Johannes-burg, in 2008, and South Africa vs Australia, also Johannesburg, in 2009 – before I stood in five of the ICC World Twenty20 matches in England during the middle of 2009. The tournament was won by Pakistan, who beat Sri Lanka in the final.

The star of the show was undoubtedly Tillakaratne Dilshan, who scored 317 runs at an average of 52. He showed what a dan-gerous opener and innovative batsman he is, covering the full

360 degrees of the field with paddles and scoops and reverse sweeps – you name it. In the semi-final against the West Indies he hit a spectacular, unbeaten 96 to give Sri Lanka a defendable target.

Chris Gayle was another player who gripped the imagination, scoring 193 runs at an average of 48. He was mainly responsible for knocking Australia out of the competition when he smashed a brutal 88 off just 50 balls at The Oval. One of his sixes off Brett Lee landed all the way in Harleyford Road, and another ended up on top of the Bedser Pavilion! Shahid Afridi was almost as spectacular, hitting 176 runs in the tournament. He had looked oddly out of touch when he totalled just 18 runs in his first three innings, but fortunately for Pakistan he saved his best for the semi-final and final with a half-century in each. Kumar Sangakkara scored the third-most runs in the tournament with 177 runs, but his efforts weren't enough for his side to win the trophy.

While I'd missed out on the 2007 World Twenty20 championship because of disciplinary measures instituted against those who officiated in the 2007 World Cup final (discussed in Chapter 9), I was part of the umpiring elite at the inaugural IPL (Indian Premier League) Twenty20 series in India in 2008. I acted as on-field umpire in the very first match (the Bangalore Royal Challengers vs the Kolkata Knight Riders), as well as in the final of the tournament (the Chennai Super Kings vs the Rajasthan Royals), among other matches.

I can't recall a ball ever being whacked around a cricket field as much as in the Kolkata Knight Riders' innings at Bangalore. They had three of the world's best batsmen at the top of their order: Ganguly, Brendon McCullum and Ponting. But it was McCullum who set the tournament ablaze with 158 runs off just 73 balls, a strike rate of 216 per cent. Ten fours and 13 sixes – that's what the crowds had come for! My goodness, how the bowlers were punished. Jacques Kallis went for 48 in four overs and Craig White for 24 in his one and only over.

On paper, the Rajasthan Royals, led by Shane Warne, didn't look at all like one of the favourites at the start of the tournament, but just to prove that this means nothing in a game like Twenty20, they went all the way and won the final in Mumbai against the Chennai Super Kings, chasing 165 for victory.

I was also privileged to stand as on-field umpire in the much-publicised Stanford Superstars vs England match at the end of 2008 at the Stanford Cricket Ground, Coolidge, Antigua. There were pots of money for the players in this, the most lucrative cricket match ever played, but the England chaps surely didn't deserve any of it, as the Stanford Superstars won by 10 wickets with 44 balls remaining. England was all out for 99, and Chris Gayle only needed 45 balls to blast 65 not out.

In the middle of February 2009, Sir Allen Stanford, the Texan billionaire who had sponsored the event, was charged by the Securities and Exchange Commission of the United States with alleged investment fraud totalling $9.2 billion. By then, all cricketing bodies who had had close ties with the man had suffered enormous embarrassment. So that was the last of Stanford staging any Twenty20 matches in future.

9

The World Cup

" *As far as World Cups go, time has been running out for me, and if I don't stand in another tournament, so be it. I've had a memorable innings in the World Cups, for which I am very grateful.* **"**

The ICC Cricket World Cup is often hailed as the game's premier showpiece. Because of the fact that it is contested in the shorter version of the game, some purists may dispute that claim, but be that as it may, I was privileged to have umpired in three World Cups: in 1999, 2003 and 2007. At the 2003 World Cup I had the added honour of officiating on-field in one of the semi-finals and as third umpire in the final, and in the 2007 World Cup final as third umpire – a controversial event that all the officials will probably regret for the rest of their lives. But more about that later. I was also appointed as on-field umpire for both the 2004 and 2006 ICC Champions Trophy finals.

The 1999 World Cup, held in England, kicked off with a match between the hosts and Sri Lanka at Lord's, and it being my first World Cup, I was delighted to be appointed to stand in this very first game of the tournament – especially since it was being played at that wonderful venue. I recall it being a very one-sided match, England winning by eight wickets, much to the joy of the home crowd, of course. I also stood in the fifth Super Six game, between Australia and Zimbabwe, also at Lord's, in which the Aussies scored just over 300 runs, thanks to the Waugh brothers. Despite a brave 152 by Neil Johnson, the Zimbabweans were well short of the target.

What a joy it was for me to have stood twice at Lord's. At some stage, the other umpires jokingly referred to me as 'Lord Koertzen'! I also had the great prospect of returning to Lord's three weeks later for a Test between England and New Zealand, which would be my first Test at this famous ground – and, fortunately, not my last.

We had some 'fun' at Headingley, where I stood in the Pool B game between Australia and Pakistan, who would later oppose each other in the final. Set a target of 276, Australia stayed on course for most of the match, but eventually finished 10 runs short. There was a lot of pressure on both sides, and it showed in the game. A simmering feeling of aggression between Australian skipper Steve Waugh and the fiery Shoaib Akhtar – at that stage the quickest bowler in the world – erupted when Waugh drove a delivery from Akhtar past the bowler and crossed for a run. In his follow-through, a frustrated Akhtar kicked at Waugh. I immediately realised that the situation had to be nipped in the bud and I told the upset Waugh that I would handle it.

I then spoke to Akhtar. 'We're playing cricket, here, not soccer,' I told him. I also spoke to the Pakistan captain, Wasim Akram, and asked him to tell his team to cool it. I was happy that the matter had been resolved on the field, and left it at that. The match referee, Raman Subba Row, also spoke to Akhtar later.

Pakistan were the favourites to win the tournament, especially after beating the Kiwis by nine wickets in their semi-final. But what a disappointment the other semi-final between the Aussies and South Africa, and then the final between Australia and Pakistan after that, turned out to be. South Africans still cry in their beers after that heart-breaking run-out of Allan Donald with the scores tied at 213.

A memorable moment – and probably a turning point – in the South Africa/Australia semi-final, especially from a South African point of view, was when Herschelle Gibbs caught Steve Waugh when he still had a low score, but lost control of the ball as he tossed it in the air in a reflex movement. Waugh said something like, 'You've just dropped the World Cup, son,' and how true that turned out to be!

In the final, Pakistan was simply outplayed by the Aussies, and only managed 132 runs, with Warnie spinning his magic to take four wickets. And when opener Adam Gilchrist reached his 50 after only 33 balls, there could have been only one result. Poor Shoaib Akhtar went for over nine runs an over, Azhar Mamood for 10 an over, and Steve Waugh's men won by eight wickets with 179 balls to spare. Watching Gilchrist batting, I always wondered what the poor bowler running up to him must be thinking. How often did what looked like a good ball suddenly disappear into the crowd! Where the heck is one supposed to bowl? But at least, from a bowler's perspective, there was always a chance that with Gillie's approach he could get out at any time.

A feature of the 1999 tournament was the great number of wides that were bowled, and perhaps for two reasons: the Duke ball that the bowlers used swung more than usual, and we as umpires were a bit stricter on the chaps than before. It's interesting to note that in the Pakistan innings in the final, Extras top-scored with 25 (13 wides, two no-balls and 10 leg byes). Ijaz Ahmed, who was bowled by Warne on 22, was the only batsman to exceed 20 runs.

The next World Cup, in 2003, was hosted by South Africa, Zimbabwe and Kenya, and the number of teams increased from 12 to 14. During the tournament, I reached a personal milestone when I stood in my 100th ODI in the semi-final between Australia and Sri Lanka in Port Elizabeth, with the experienced Dave Shepherd as my co-umpire. To have achieved that in front of my home crowd was the cherry on the cake for me.

Kenya turned out to be the surprise packet of the tournament, beating both Sri Lanka and Zimbabwe. They were also helped along when New Zealand forfeited a match by refusing to play in Kenya because of security concerns, thus enabling the Kenyans to reach the semi-finals. Of course everyone thought that South Africa, and not any of the other teams from Africa, would be in the semis, as they were obviously one of the favourites to win the tournament – but Shaun Pollock's men didn't make it to the last four.

As in 1999, it was crying time again for the Proteas and the local fans. South Africa, after being trounced by New Zealand, met Sri Lanka in a do-or-die match in Durban. At that stage the Sri Lankans weren't too hot either, having lost to Kenya. Just to jog readers' memories: Set a target of 269, the Proteas innings had its ups and downs, but a good partnership between captain Shaun Pollock and Mark Boucher set them on course for victory – until Pollock was run out with a steady drizzle coming down. As the rain increased, it became clear that the game would end prematurely. So, at the end of the 44th over, the Proteas dressing room sent a message to Boucher, out at the crease with Lance Klusener, that, according to the Duckworth-Lewis system, they needed 229 by the end of the next over. Boucher hit a six off the penultimate ball of the over to take the score to 229, and pleased that he had won the game, just defended the last ball. In now heavy rain, the umpires – Bucknor and Venkataraghavan – took the players off.

But lo and behold, the instructions from the dressing room had been wrong. The Proteas' 229 runs guaranteed them a tie, not a win, which was what they needed to go through to the Super Six. Heartbreak took over from elation. Poor Shaun Pollock. He had to endure the fury of a hugely disappointed South African public, and was later sacked as captain, making way for Graeme Smith.

I stood in the Aussies' semi-final against Sri Lanka at my home ground, St George's Park, where Gilchrist exhibited a wonderful show of sportsmanship. Although most people agreed that what he'd done was admirable, his skipper, Ricky Ponting, and his team-mates were less than thrilled. Gillie was batting at an ominous 20 off 22 balls when the Sri Lankans appealed for a caught behind to Kumar Sangakkara off Aravinda de Silva's bowling. I didn't think Gillie had nicked it, but just as I was saying 'not out', he walked off anyway, astounding his dressing room, the Sri Lankans and most of the spectators. What could I do? Call him back? In such a situation, an umpire is powerless to stop a batsman.

After the match Ponting said that all the players in the dressing room were taken by surprise when their teammate walked. And he added that he wouldn't encourage them to follow Gilchrist's example: don't give up your wicket until the umpire has raised his finger.

Of course the Sri Lankans were only too happy that Gilchrist had walked, and they applauded the fact that there were 'still some gentlemen in the game'. And one has to admit, for a batsman to walk is very rare these days.

In the final between Australia and India at the Wanderers in Johannesburg, Australia made 359 runs, the largest-ever total in a final, and lost only two wickets. I watched the game from my position as TV umpire. Gilchrist was again the man who set Australia on course to victory when he hit 57 off 48 balls, helped along magnificently by Ponting, who scored 140 unbeaten runs. Australia's 359 runs were always going to be a massive target for India to reach, and in the end Ponting's men won by 125 runs – a big win for a final.

Four years later, Australia made it three in a row when they beat Sri Lanka in the World Cup final. But it was the five officials in the 2007 final, me included, and the sad death of Pakistan coach Bob Woolmer that grabbed the attention of the world more than the actual cricket.

The tournament was hosted by the West Indies, thus making the Cricket World Cup the first such tournament to be hosted on all six continents. I reached another ODI milestone during this tournament when I equalled Dave Shepherd's record of 172 appearances. To have found myself in the company of an umpiring legend like Dave Shepherd in sharing the record was indeed a great privilege for me. My next target was to become the first umpire to stand in 200 ODIs, which I had to wait until 2009 to achieve.

Two of the minnows of world cricket, Bangladesh and Ireland, fared unexpectedly well in the 2007 World Cup. Bangladesh progressed to the second round for the first time, after defeating one of the tournament favourites, India, and they went on to show that it was no fluke when they defeated South Africa in the second round. Ireland made their World Cup debut, and tied with Zimbabwe and then defeated Pakistan – quite appropriately on St Patrick's Day! – to go through to the second round. Their defeat of Pakistan was surely one of the biggest upsets in the history of the tournament, and it effectively knocked the Pakistanis out of the World Cup. Ireland also went on to defeat Bangladesh and were promoted to the main ODI table.

On the Sunday after Ireland had defeated Pakistan, we were stunned by the news that the Pakistan coach, Bob Woolmer, had been found unconscious in his room in the Jamaica Pegasus Hotel in Kingston and was later pronounced dead at the local hospital. To top it all, the Jamaican police announced that he had been strangled.

Ironically, thousands of kilometres away in Pakistan, on the Saturday of Pakistan's defeat and a day before Woolmer's death, fans had been baying for his blood, shouting 'Death to Bob Woolmer!' and burning his effigy in the streets of Multan. But I think even the most fanatical among them would have been shocked by the news of his death.

The match-fixing scandal was still fresh in people's minds, and for years rumours had followed the Pakistan team. Not surprisingly, conspiracy theories abounded: the match against Ireland was 'thrown' and the bookmakers' Mafia were involved in Woolmer's

The Despatch High School U14 cricket team, 1963. I am sitting on the floor on the right. Author Chris Schoeman is sitting behind me. Our coach (left) is Mr Christo Swart and the principal is Mr JN Coetzee

The Despatch High School First XI, 1965. I am standing on the far left in the back row. Chris is seated third from left, front row. Same coach, same principal

Our wedding day in my hometown, 2 May 1970

Walking off the Kingsmead pitch with Hansie Cronjé after the South Africa vs India final of the Standard Bank ODI series in 1997

Trying to calm the fiery tempers of Shoaib Akhtar and Steve Waugh
at Headingley during the 1999 World Cup

Walking onto Lord's with Doug Cowie during the 1999 World Cup

Watching a delivery by Australia's Michael Bevan during their Super Six match against Zimbabwe at Lord's during the 1999 World Cup

Caught by the camera after ducking for a hook shot in the controversial South Africa vs England Test at Centurion in 2000

Knocking in the stumps while Sachin Tendulkar appeals to the crowd to stop moving behind the bowler's arm during a World Cup match between India and England at Kingsmead in 2003

Getting ready for my 100th ODI with Dave Shepherd: the 2003 World Cup semi-final between Australia and Sri Lanka in Port Elizabeth

Slow death to an Aussie batsman during their Test match against the World XI in Sydney, 14 October 2005

A lighter moment with Shivnarine Chanderpaul and Ramnaresh Sarwan at Hobart during the second Test of the Frank Worrall Trophy series, November 2005

The ultimate pressure. A typical Shane Warne appeal, supported by Ricky Ponting and Matthew Hayden

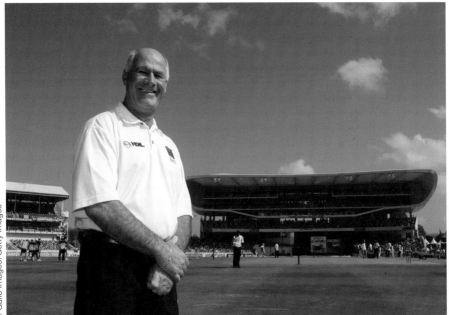

During the 2007 World Cup, I equalled Dave Shepherd's record of 172 ODIs in the West Indies vs Bangladesh Super Eight match at the Kensington Oval, Bridgetown, Barbados, on 19 April

Sharing a joke with Brian Lara during his last ever international innings, in the World Cup match against England at Kensington Oval, 21 April 2007

Giving a batsman the green light as third umpire in the first Test between New Zealand and the West Indies in Dunedin, 14 December 2008

Shaking hands with England captain Andrew Strauss on the fifth day of the third Ashes Test in Birmingham, 3 August 2009

death. There was talk that he had been in the final stages of writing a book, and that it probably contained sensational revelations. After all, he had been Hansie Cronjé's coach for five years prior to 2000, when the Proteas captain was found guilty of match fixing.

After Hansie was banned for life, Woolmer bemoaned the fact that his captain had had too much power and as a result had thought himself invulnerable. Apparently Hansie had gradually assumed more and more control as the United Cricket Board – and particularly Dr Ali Bacher – gave him increasing power. Woolmer, as coach, Hansie, as captain, and Peter Pollock, as convener of selectors (and a man of great integrity), were the only three who decided on team selection and tactics. But Woolmer denied any match throwing during the 1999 World Cup, describing the loss to Zimbabwe as merely a 'bad day at the office'.

At the time of Woolmer's death he had been coaching the Pakistan side for three years. Before the Pakistan team could return home, each player had to provide a DNA sample, was fingerprinted and individually questioned. Woolmer's death cast a shadow over the tournament, which was supposed to have been a joyous celebration in the colourful Caribbean. As security was stepped up, the atmosphere grew increasingly gloomy. One of our umpires was in the Pegasus Hotel when a clap of thunder suddenly made him rush outside, his first thought being that a bomb had gone off.

Even though the Jamaican police confirmed a murder investigation into Woolmer's death based on the government pathologist's report that he had been strangled, three months later it was concluded that he had died of natural causes. Three independent pathologists and Scotland Yard detectives, who had travelled to Jamaica for the investigation, reported that he had suffered from diabetes and an enlarged heart, which may have contributed to his death. I had met Bob on occasion, but I can't say that I'd known him well. But people in cricketing circles who had been close to him have no doubt that the finding was correct.

While some people took delight in Pakistan and India's untimely exits, their departures had a negative impact on the tournament. Apart from the consequences to commercial interests, their absence robbed the 2007 World Cup of several of its stars who could have set the stage alight. When the tournament got to a point where some fireworks were required, gone were Inzamam-ul-Haq and Mohammad Yousuf, Sachin Tendulkar and Mahendra Dhoni. Of course one had to be happy for Ireland and Bangladesh for achieving the unexpected, but to be honest, their players simply did not have the same appeal as the stars I've just mentioned.

Although they avoided first-round elimination, the subsequent failure of the West Indies and England further deflated interest. The England players had suffered severe consequences when, on the night after losing to New Zealand in their opening fixture, they'd rather excessively enjoyed the attractions of St Lucia. Andrew Flintoff was suspended for one match and stripped of his vice-captaincy after capsizing a pedalo in the sea near the team's hotel in the early hours of the morning. Apparently he'd had to be rescued by a security guard. In addition, his teammates James Anderson, Ian Bell, Jon Lewis, Paul Nixon and Liam Plunkett were fined for a 'breach of team discipline' when photos of them behaving drunkenly in a bar appeared in the press. The pictures had been taken by fans on their mobile phones.

The South African side had entered the tournament as one of the favourites. Herschelle Gibbs took advantage of the small dimensions of Warner Park in St Kitts, hitting Dutch spinner Daan van Bunge for six sixes in one over, a feat previously achieved by the great Gary Sobers and Ravi Shastri in first-class cricket, but never in an international match. The South Africans then had a close escape against Sri Lanka (when Lasith Malinga took four wickets with consecutive balls) and had the humiliation of losing to Bangladesh for the first time in their eight clashes up to that stage. They also lost to New Zealand, which was no disgrace, but still made it to the semi-final. But that was as far as they got.

The efficient Aussies simply bundled them out of the tournament, adding credence to the claim that the Proteas were 'chokers', a tag they've carried since their return to international cricket in 1991/92.

There was no doubt that Australia had been the team of the tournament. They won all of their matches and topped both the batting and bowling lists. Matthew Hayden's 659 runs were only 14 short of Sachin Tendulkar's 2003 World Cup record, while Ponting also passed 500. Australia's bowling was just as balanced, and included seamers such as McGrath, Shaun Tait and Nathan Bracken, and spinner Brad Hogg. McGrath, in his fourth and final World Cup, took his overall tally to 71 wickets, easily eclipsing Wasim Akram's previous record of 55. The Aussies also looked sharper and fitter in the field than any other team, and overall they were the most consistent.

About halfway through the 2007 World Cup tournament I started thinking that I had had enough of it. I had arrived in the West Indies two weeks before the start of the tournament, and by then I was fed up and just wanted to go home. Surely four weeks should be long enough to complete the World Cup? (But more on those thoughts later.) Well, if only I could have gone home when I felt like it, I would have been spared the embarrassment of the final!

From a spectator's point of view, the match between England and the West Indies was arguably the best match of the sometimes boring seven weeks. The Kensington Oval ground was packed to capacity in spite of the fact that the semi-finalists had already been settled and that neither of the two sides was among them. Fortunes fluctuated, and victory for England only came off the penultimate ball of the match. The crowd also experienced the spectacle of saying farewell to the incomparable Brian Lara, whom I had the privilege of watching play his majestic strokes over many years. Some consolation for England were the hard-hit hundreds Kevin Pietersen scored against Australia and the West Indies, with which he proved himself once again as one of the most destructive players in the modern game.

And so Ponting's men eliminated the Proteas and Sri Lanka took care of New Zealand in their respective semi-finals for Australia to face Sri Lanka in the final on Saturday 28 April. Steve Bucknor and Aleem Dar were the two on-field umpires, I the third umpire, Billy Bowden the reserve official and former New Zealand captain Jeff Crowe the match referee. Steve was standing in a record fifth successive World Cup final – quite a remarkable feat.

Proceedings started off on the wrong foot when we had to reduce the match to 38 overs a side because of rain. Ironically, the ICC had been worried about the unpredictable Caribbean weather towards the end of May, thus pushing the original tournament dates back by a month – only for the rain to upset proceedings on the most important morning of the tournament! Reducing the overs was an unsatisfactory and disappointing way of determining one-day cricket's most prestigious prize of all, but there you go … At least Adam Gilchrist's phenomenal batting that followed held some consolation for the crowd of 20 000, as did Jayasuriya and Sangakkara's fightback in the first part of the Sri Lankan innings.

Ricky Ponting's men took off like a house on fire, and at the drinks break, after 19 overs, the score was already 135 for no wicket. When Matthew Hayden had only 30, Gilchrist was already on 95, and he went on to make 149 off just 104 balls. Australia finished on 281/4, at more than seven runs per over. Sri Lanka really had their work cut out for them.

Jayasuriya and Sangakkara tried bravely with a second-wicket stand of 116, scoring a 50 each, but Sri Lanka's effort effectively ended once these two batsmen got out within three overs of each other. The team's resistance crumbled, and then more rain reduced their number of overs to 36. At the end of the 33rd over, with Sri Lanka still needing almost 70 runs off three overs, the light was so poor that it was offered to the batsmen, who accepted and walked off. Believing they had already won, the Aussies started celebrating. And quite rightly so.

However, back in the stand, we, the match officials, cut their victory dances short, as we had decided that the last three overs had to be played out. Law 21 states that, providing a minimum of 20 overs have been played, a result can be reached using the Duckworth-Lewis method. Ponting and Sri Lankan captain Mahela Jayawardene then mutually decided to finish the three overs, in which only spinners would be used. The rest of the game was played in very poor light, Australia finally winning by 53 runs (D/L method).

Ponting admitted after the match that it had been embarrassing to go back onto the field after they had already started celebrating their win, and that it had been disappointing that the match had ended in such a way. I can only agree. Jayawardene added that, in spite of all the confusion, the result had never been in doubt. His side could not have won the game, and Australia deserved to win, given the way in which they had played.

Up until the final, the tournament had passed without any major criticism of the umpires. But after the confusion of the last overs, we were blamed for generating 'a farcical conclusion to the tournament'. The spectators, of course, were very upset too, and it was a bit embarrassing when they booed us during the trophy presentation ceremony. But that's life …

Jeff Crowe later blamed a 'communication breakdown' between him, me and on-field umpires Aleem Dar and Steve Bucknor for the mix-up, and said that it should never have happened. Jeff took the blame, but he also implied that I may have started the process that had led to the confusion.

'In hindsight,' Crowe told the media, 'I should have known the rules and said the game had been called off. I'm very embarrassed for the playing control team today. I think the real confusion has come from the fact [that] we were talking about resuming the game tomorrow, which was technically wrong. Sometimes you get a stronger voice which says: "I know the rules – this is how it works." Then you get a bit of confusion in the group itself, and no one wants to overrule the other. The match referee should have known and said, "That's not right – the game should be completed now."'

Crowe said that I had mentioned 'allowances' and the possibility of resuming play the next day, but he went on to say that he didn't think it was 'Rudi's mistake; it's a collective mistake. The fact [that] Rudi might have suggested it early doesn't mean the other umpires couldn't have overruled him. The two on-field umpires are the ones who control the match.'

So, as the decision to continue the game had been taken by all the umpires, I don't think anyone could be singled out for blame. The fact remains that we should have stopped the match, but the circumstances caught us completely off-guard. Everybody makes mistakes, and we made a mistake by allowing the match to continue. I have since thought about the situation a lot, and I still don't know how it could have happened. But unfortunately, and understandably, the matter put a damper on the final.

Then again, in the final of the 2004 Championship Trophy in England the light conditions were even poorer, but the match was completed because the players and 35 000 spectators insisted on it.

In the end, we, the five officials in the 2007 World Cup final, were reprimanded and made to pay the price for our mistake. Two months after the World Cup, the ICC boss, Malcolm Speed, announced that all of us were suspended from officiating in the 2007 ICC World Twenty20 championship. 'It would have been easy to let sleeping dogs lie and pretend nothing happened,' he said, 'but the reality is that the playing control team made a serious and fundamental error that caused the final of our flagship event to end in disarray and confusion. That was not acceptable for such experienced and talented officials, and although we do not like to have to take such action, we felt it necessary to decline to appoint them for our next event, the ICC World Twenty20 in South Africa.'

Crowe, in reaction to this decision, said, 'While it is never easy to take criticism, I think it is right that there are consequences for our actions as match officials. In this instance I understand that the ICC could not merely let it go.' I'm sure the rest of us who officiated in the final agreed.

In the end, the tournament had dragged on for 47 days, which was as long as the last Olympic Games and FIFA World Cup put together. Once the number of teams had been increased from 14 (in 2003) to 16, and reserve days in case of bad weather introduced, it was always going to be a long, drawn-out affair. Proteas coach Mickey Arthur complained that his team had to hang around for seven days between their final game of the Super 8 and the semi-final, and that they lost momentum as a result – by no means a far-fetched statement.

By the time of the next World Cup, in 2011, I will probably have retired. It seems, at least, that the ICC have learnt from the experiences of the past World Cup tournaments. They have allocated the 2011 World Cup to its four Asian members – Bangladesh, India, Pakistan and Sri Lanka – but following the security problems in Pakistan, they probably won't be in the mix.

The even greater distances that will need to be covered in Asia and the potential political issues could be of some concern to the ICC and the event organisers. But fortunately they have recognised that the last tournament went on for too long. ICC CEO Malcolm Speed indicated that the ICC will try to reduce the next World Cup by between seven and 10 days. It remains to be seen how this is going to be effectively implemented, however, as the ICC are again planning to enter 16 teams. They have at all times defended their inclusion of so many minor teams, but Ricky Ponting's opinion is that these teams' entry into the tournament should be conditional on them dominating the lower international tiers over a period of time. 'I would like to see them prove themselves the best of the emerging group by quite a way,' he said, and this should happen 'over a two-year period, not [in] one tournament'.

Many share his opinion. One of my lasting memories of the 2007 World Cup is of how one-sided most of the matches had been, one following another, and the players from the stronger sides obviously growing bored. According to the stats, six of the matches were won by more than 200 runs (which is a hell of a lot for a one-dayer!), of which five involved Bermuda, Holland and Scotland. Another six matches were won by more than 100 runs. No fewer than 16 matches were won with seven or more wickets to spare, and only three went into the last over. So the question the ICC have to ask themselves is whether or not the associated countries devalue the World Cup tournament. After all, it is cricket's premier event.

As far as World Cups go, time has been running out for me, and if I don't stand in another tournament, so be it. I've had a memorable innings in the World Cups, for which I am very grateful.

10

Match fixing

"At the time, if you had asked me for the names of a hundred people who I thought might be involved in cricket corruption, Hansie's would not have been among them. When his involvement in the match-fixing scandal was exposed, I couldn't believe what I was hearing."

In September 1999, I was staying in a hotel in Singapore while officiating in the Coca-Cola Challenge between the West Indies, Zimbabwe and India, when, on the day before the final, the phone rang in my room. The man on the other end of the line told me how he had been following my career for a long time, and that as far as he was concerned, I was the best umpire in the business. Of course it's nice to hear those things, but then he added that he was coming to the hotel where I was staying, and that he would like to chat to me about the next day's game between India and the West Indies.

That's okay, I said, I would meet him in the foyer of the hotel if he wanted to talk. No, he replied, he would like to talk to me in my hotel room. When I insisted that we meet in the foyer, he repeated that he would rather talk in my room. I immediately started to suspect something fishy and put the phone down.

A little while later, the same bloke phoned. He apologised for troubling me again, but said he would really like to talk to me about the next day's match. Convinced that I was talking to a bookmaker, I told him that I wasn't interested in bribes and match fixing, and put the phone down. He didn't call again, but I never-theless reported the incident to Brian Basson, who was then heading the South African Umpires Association, as well as Dr Ali Bacher at the UCBSA.

And so ended my first, and to date my only, experience with a bookie.

This kind of phone call, of course, wasn't without precedent. Five years before, in 1994, another South African umpire, Cyril Mitchley, was approached by a bookmaker who offered him $50 000 to help manipulate the outcome of a Test from behind the stumps.

Cricket has always been highly popular with gamblers and bookmakers for betting on, as the nature of the game offers them endless possibilities and permutations. They can bet on runs scored by an individual batsman, or the team collectively, the number of runs scored in the first 20 overs, the number of fours or sixes, or the number of runs a bowler will concede. These are just some of the possibilities. For bookmakers the game has the added advantage of lasting for a long time; if bookmakers see that bets are running against them, they can try to reverse their fortunes by laying bets in favour of the opposing proposition.

The year before I was approached, it was revealed that two of Australia's top players, Mark Waugh and Shane Warne, had been implicated in match-fixing practices. It was revealed that a few years earlier they had accepted money from a person known only as 'John' in return for information on the pitch and weather conditions. Both Waugh and Warne insisted that the informa-tion they had given had been restricted to these two factors, which bookmakers could have acquired from advance television coverage anyway.

But it wasn't that simple: both Waugh and Warne were cricket idols, role models for the youngsters and much sought-after by the game's sponsors. Suddenly the world was forced to acknowledge cricket's ties with unscrupulous bookmakers. And had the book-makers a special strategy in mind when they approached these two players in particular? Both Waugh and Warne were known to be keen gamblers, Waugh's special passion being horse racing. Because these two guys loved to bet, they had become targets and were approached for what could be regarded as an easy dollar.

Then, in November 1999, the Justice Qayyum Report on alleged match fixing among the Pakistan players was released to the Pakistan Cricket Board, recommending that Salim Malik be banned for life.

Soon afterwards, on 7 April 2000, South Africa was rocked when news broke that four South African players had been impli-cated in match-fixing activities during the one-day series in India. Delhi police reports named Hansie Cronjé, Nicky Bojé, Herschelle Gibbs and Pieter Strydom as the alleged guilty parties. Dr Bacher subsequently issued a statement saying that he had spoken to all four players, and that they emphatically denied that there was any substance to the allegations.

I was as stunned as the public, and on the evening of Bacher's statement, listeners called in to a special TV programme to sup-port Hansie. One cricket fan said he'd believe the Pope was a bigamist before he believed Hansie was involved in bribery and corruption. Fans simply adored him. His dark side, it seemed, was well hidden in spite of him being constantly in the public eye. Of course, what goes for Hansie can go for other cricketing heroes too.

When Delhi police released the taped conversation between Hansie and one Sanjay Chawla, a blacklisted bookie, some people dismissed it out of hand, but, quite significantly, Kepler Wessels – who would have got to know about these things in his many years in international cricket – cautioned that match fixing was rife in the game, and that the UCBSA would be making a big mistake if they tried to sweep the allegations under the carpet without investigating them properly.

A court of inquiry under the chairmanship of Judge Edwin King was set up, and, under severe pressure, Hansie admitted to throwing matches and that other Proteas players had also been involved. He was immediately banned from all cricket. The UCBSA also fined Herschelle Gibbs and Henry Williams and suspended both from international cricket for six months. No other South African players were punished in connection with the scandal, in spite of the fact that some of them had been withholding information for years.

Hansie also implicated Salim Malik, as well as Mohammad Azharuddin and Ajay Jadeja of India, who were subsequently banned from all cricket. After the conclusion of the inquiry, everyone was convinced that a great deal had *not* been revealed. Hansie's untimely death in a plane crash in 2002 also helped most of his connections to escape the law.

When Hansie's role in match fixing was revealed, some fans turned into conspiracy theorists and suddenly found suspicious circumstances in various incidents that had occurred in cricket. South Africa's performance at the 1999 World Cup was one such example. They pointed to Hansie's poor showing with the bat during the tournament: 98 runs in eight innings, including two ducks in the crucial matches against Australia. They also wanted to know how the Proteas could have lost to Zimbabwe after having won all their previous matches, and recalled how Herschelle Gibbs, Hansie's co-accused in the King Commission trial, had spilt the ball when he prematurely celebrated a catch off Steve Waugh in the semi-final. And of course they pointed to the run-out that had occurred at the death to tie the match and see the Aussies go through to the final.

In his testimony before the King Commission, Hansie tried to explain how tempting it was for young players to provide 'harmless' information in exchange for, say, $50 000. Yet I don't think anybody, me included, could have guessed that a guy like Hansie would be involved in match fixing. At the time, if you had asked me for the names of a hundred people who I thought might be involved in cricket corruption, Hansie's would not have been among them.

When his involvement in the match-fixing scandal was exposed, I couldn't believe what I was hearing. It may sound naive now, but in hindsight we all have perfect vision. Who knows, if the Delhi police had not come forward with the incriminating tape-recorded conversations, Hansie may have gone on playing for many years and finished his career without the truth ever coming out …

Personally I had always got along well with Hansie. Some have said that he could be moody at times, but I can honestly say that he was never unfriendly towards me. On one occasion I was going to stop by his house in Fancourt in George but he was out of town, and he simply said, 'You know where I live … help yourself to a beer in the fridge.' That was the kind of guy he was – from my experience, anyway.

From what I saw – and I think I was close enough on the field – Hansie was one of the best international captains I'd come across in my time. He was not only tactically astute, but always the fittest and sharpest man on the team. Under Hansie's leadership, the Proteas became known as the most hard-working outfit in the international game. Now, unfortunately, we all know that he had been counting his money as well, but no one can accuse him of not having set an example in his dedication to be the best.

One of the matches in which Hansie was implicated was the fifth South Africa/England Test at Centurion, which started on 14 January 2000. Darrell Hair and I stood as on-field umpires. As mentioned in an earlier chapter, rain caused almost one and a half sessions to be lost on the first day, and South Africa finished on 155 for six. Then both the second and third days were rained out without a ball being bowled. When play finally resumed, South Africa added 93 runs before Hansie decided on a controversial declaration.

By mutual agreement, England then declared their first innings 0/0, and South Africa forfeited their second innings, as prescribed by Note 2 of Law 14, forfeiture of second innings. This left England a moderate target of 249 off 76 overs. South Africa had already wrapped up the series 2-0, so they had nothing to lose, but I couldn't help thinking that Hansie had made a generous declaration. Of course the thought of match fixing never entered my mind.

Alec Stewart and Michael Vaughan put together a big partnership of 126 for the fifth wicket, but at 240/8, England was worried again. In the meantime, a large afternoon crowd had turned up to watch an entertaining day's drama. At the death, with six needed off seven balls, Chris Silverwood hit a boundary from Pollock's last over, after which Darren Gough whacked a four off Hayward through mid-wicket for an exciting England win.

During the King Commission hearing, Hansie insisted that he had played to win, that the match had produced a genuine result and that the result had in no way been manipulated. But according to Michael Atherton, in retrospect it was easy to see that Hansie's bowling changes and field placings had been designed to prevent a draw. I've never been an international cricket captain, so I can't really comment, but former England skipper Nasser Hussain said that the Centurion Test will always be remembered for having been fixed, and that, consequently, it had ruined the England victory.

In Hansie's testimony at the King Commission hearing, it transpired that he had met with Marlon Aronstam, a professional gambler, at the Sandton Hotel on the evening of the fourth day of the Test, and they had discussed declaring in order to make a game of it. Aronstam had promised R500 000 to a charity organisation of Hansie's choice, as well as 'a present' to Hansie. On the fifth day, Hansie and Nasser Hussain agreed on a declaration and Hansie sent an SMS to Aronstam to say 'the game is on'.

Aronstam later claimed it had been too late at that stage to get bets on the match. The next evening, after the Proteas' defeat, Hansie again met Aronstam at the hotel and was handed a leather jacket and a cash amount of R30 000. The next day, he received a further R20 000. The money, Hansie explained, was not a reward for the day's result, but instead would serve as a deposit for the information he would provide on the upcoming triangular one-day series.

In 2000, when the ICC was criticised for not having a proper plan of action to counter the practice of match fixing, they appointed a former Metropolitan Police commissioner, Sir Paul Condon, to head an anti-corruption inquiry. Claims of organised match fixing went back as far as the 1970s, when bookmakers had allegedly bribed players on the 1979/80 Pakistan tour of India.

According to Condon's report, three venues had become noted for corrupt cricketing practices, namely the desert ground of Sharjah, where matches had been played since 1984, and Toronto and Singapore. I was not surprised at the mention of Singapore, because that was where I was approached by a bookmaker. Condon described the 'relaxed regimes' under which corrupt practices took place in a 'carnival atmosphere', and that one of the trademarks of these tournaments was an absence of competitive urgency. According to Recommendation No. 9 of the report: 'If commercial imperatives continue to take international matches to neutral venues such as Sharjah, Canada, Singapore or elsewhere the ICC must recognize that the relaxed carnival atmosphere and the blurred regimes for payments and gifts provide an ideal venue for improper approaches. Extra vigilance and security will be necessary if these neutral venues continue to be used or expanded.'

Other factors that contributed to corruption included cricket players being paid less than other top athletes, such as soccer players and golfers; a lack of security at hotels, training grounds and stadia, which allowed for unrestricted mixing between players, supporters and journalists; and tournaments in which national pride was not at stake.

Condon's report outlined international cricket-betting corruption over a period of at least 20 years, but claimed that the establishment and investigations of the anti-corruption unit and other recent measures had stopped much of the illegal activities. The report also mentioned that many people within the game had significant information on corruption practices, but were afraid of the repercussions if they spoke out. Some had been threatened, while others had linked murder and kidnapping to cricket corruption.

Furthermore, in November 2000 India's Central Bureau of Investigation reported that the underground cricket Mafia were rumoured to have taken over control of the betting racket, and that what had started as small-time wagering was now being run by an organised syndicate. Eventually, the match-fixing allegations of recent years came to a head during the 2007 ICC Cricket World Cup. Prompted by the sudden and suspicious death of Pakistan's coach Bob Woolmer shortly after Pakistan had lost to Ireland and been bundled out of the tournament, the Jamaican police opened a murder investigation. This came as no surprise, as Pakistan has often been accused of throwing matches.

In 1994 the team had to swear on the Koran that they had had no part in sports betting in Australia, and the following year bookmakers refused to pay out after Pakistan's first-Test innings defeat to Zimbabwe. As recently as October 2009, the head of Pakistan's national parliamentary committee on sports, Jamshed Khan Dasti, made allegations of match fixing when Pakistan lost to New Zealand and Australia respectively in the ICC Champions Trophy (hosted by South Africa). Both Pakistan captain Younis Khan and coach Intikhab Alam vehemently denied that the matches had been fixed and expressed their disappointment and shock at the allegations. Younis was so upset he offered to resign as skipper.

Pakistan Cricket Board chairman Ijaz Butt rubbished the claims, pointing out that Pakistan had lost to Australia off the final ball of the match and that it had been a closely fought semi-final against New Zealand. Any suggestion of match fixing was thus absurd. He also reprimanded PCB council member Dr Mohammad Ali Shah for criticising the performance of Australian umpire Simon Taufel in Pakistan's match against New Zealand. Dr Shah had wanted Taufel, who was voted best umpire in the world five years in a row, banned from umpiring international matches for making 'awful' decisions.

In January 2010, IPL boss Lalit Modi excluded players from selection to the IPL who were allegedly involved in match fixing in the defunct ICL. One of the implicated players was former New Zealand international Chris Cairns. Following Cairns's exclusion from the IPL player auction, Modi posted comments on match fixing on his private Twitter account that later appeared on a well-known cricket website.

An Indian newspaper reported that ICL officials had confronted Cairns's Chandigarh Lions following their clash with the Hyderabad Heroes, telling the players that they had 'evidence' to prove that they had deliberately underperformed. Apparently some team members then confessed, but Cairns and Dinesh Mongia denied everything and challenged the ICL to prove the allegations. In January 2010, Cairns announced plans to sue Modi, who, in an interview, responded, 'Let him sue us, then we will produce what we have to in court.'

Modi obviously seems to believe that bookies had fixed matches in the ICL, and by signing up players (and umpires!) prepared to get involved, they can easily manipulate a match. I have stood in those kinds of matches and things happen very fast: runs flow, wickets tumble and all kinds of action take place. In the pandemonium, no one has any time to bother with what happened when. Although I am not saying match fixing happened, circumstances were certainly conducive for it to happen. Bookies take bets on just about any aspect of the game: on teams, on runs, on the number of lbws, on who will win the toss ... the possibilities are endless. In the process, a player with little or no conscience can earn lots of dollars.

And, as we have seen, there *are* players with soft underbellies. Ones we would never even suspect, like Hansie, for example. And once in the grip of the bookies, they cannot escape. But bookies will always be with the game. Modi and the IPL – and the Indian Cricket Board, for that matter – will have to guard against these crooks now infiltrating the IPL, as with the ICL out of the way, the IPL will be the bookies' obvious new target. Modi's exclusion of alleged fixers from the IPL auction will not deter them. In an effort to curb fixing, the IPL has enlisted the ICC's anti-corruption unit to run a full-scale operation at their matches for 2010. The fact that the ICC saw it necessary to send the head of the unit, Ravi Sawani, to Christchurch to brief players and officials ahead of the 2010 U/19 World Cup indicates how serious matters have become.

In conclusion, I can only imagine that it will be very difficult for the world's cricketing authorities to completely stamp out corruption. Some people will always be tempted when they are offered the opportunity to make big and easy money.

11

Technology takes over

" *Once again, I was disappointed by the attitude of batsmen who refuse to walk when they know they've nicked the ball. It's a shame the way they go about it. A batsman will nick the ball, then stand there and wait for the umpires to make the decision. To me, that's nothing but cheating.* **"**

Over the years, TV technology has made big strides, and the role of technology in umpiring decisions has increased dramatically. If you look at the TV pictures from 25 years ago, they look primitive compared to what one sees on the screen today. Those pictures were grainy and the replays jerky. Worst of all, TV coverage was limited to only one end of the ground, so every other over was viewed from behind the wicketkeeper. And there were only a few cameras, whereas these days there are more than 30, showing the game from all kinds of different angles. Sometimes a camera is even hidden in the stumps and can follow the bowler in his run-up. The pictures are incredibly sharp, there are numerous replays of a wicket falling, Snickometers and graphics indicate the trajectory of the ball on the pitch, and there are even stump microphones.

The revolutionary Hawk-Eye was introduced in 2001. A gadget based on missile-guidance systems, it uses six small cameras around the ground to monitor the trajectory, speed and movement of the ball. Fed this information, a computer almost instantly produces an exact replay (or so they say) of the ball in virtual reality, showing the predicted path of the ball if it hadn't hit the batsman's pad or bat.

At the time, Hawk-Eye was a fairly radical innovation and many people disapproved of it, believing it would take away the soul of the game if the element of uncertainty was eliminated. By 2002 an electronic device – similar to the bleeper in tennis – which signals that a no-ball has just been bowled, was already available, but it has not yet been introduced. So, with all these innovations, if you as umpire make the wrong decision, it's there for the whole world to see – and criticise you like hell for it!

Umpires around the world initially thought these innovations would increasingly usurp their roles, leaving them out in the middle to perform basic functions like counting six balls to the over! I'm positive, however, that the eye of TV will not spell the end of umpires, and umpires will still be around 10 or 20 years from now. I think the day that umpires out in the middle are abolished and the running of the game is completely left to officials watching TV monitors is the day cricket will cease to be a sport. Cricket's credibility rests largely on impartial umpires, and we also contribute a lot to the emotion in the game. Imagine a match without the sight of a batsman staring incredulously, or sometimes even in disgust, at the umpire's raised finger, or a bowler glaring at an umpire for not giving an lbw, as if to say, 'You idiot, I would have knocked all three stumps out of the ground!'

Television has undoubtedly illuminated and enhanced the game of cricket; it helps to explain all the intricate strategies of the game and it makes the game easier for viewers to appreciate. But for the viewer to see exactly what's happened on television without the umpires being privy to the same information was simply unacceptable. As a result, TV technology was gradually introduced to make the umpires' job easier and help them to arrive at the right decision. It has, of course, not been absolutely foolproof, but technology has come a long way since the days when umpires only had the naked eye and no help from replays to adjudge their decisions.

I have been involved in quite a few 'firsts' in the use of TV technology. In my first Test match (South Africa vs India, Port Elizabeth, 1992), television replays were used for the first time to assist in umpiring decisions, igniting a debate that still rages on today. In September 2002, when Australian umpire Daryl Harper asked me for a review in the Pakistan/Sri Lanka Test in Colombo, I became the first TV umpire in cricket history to whom an lbw decision was referred.

Then, in October 2005 in Australia, I was the TV umpire in the first match of the Super Series, during which all decisions, including lbws and catches, were referred to the TV umpire in an ICC experiment. And in July 2008, I was third umpire when, for the first time ever, a player could challenge an on-field umpire's decision. In this instance, Indian captain Anil Kumble contested a turned-down appeal for lbw against Sri Lanka's Malinda Warnapurna, and I adjudged the first-ever referral.

South Africa introduced replay decisions for run-outs and stumpings as far back as 1992, and it was instantly beneficial. At the time I thought of the many players who had been given out over the years who had not been out, and who were given not out when they were out, before the introduction of TV replays. What influence did these incorrect decisions have on the batsman and his team's score, and on the results of matches? Judging run-outs when batsmen and ball are travelling at high speed and in opposite directions was never an easy task, but at least today we can judge to within a millimetre.

In 1993 a third umpire with two-way radio communication was employed in the Ashes series in order to assist umpires in their aim for 100 per cent accuracy. And so it went on.

In 1998, TV's third umpire was given additional responsibilities in the Standard Bank League domestic competition in South Africa. The new system was introduced during Western Province's game against North West in Fochville at the start of the competition, and the third umpire now also had to adjudge catching and lbw decisions, as well as the usual run-out, stumping and line decisions. The UCBSA were to use the experiment in all domestic matches televised by SuperSport.

I remember that, at the time, the majority on the panel of umpires at the Commonwealth Games had been in favour of technological assistance, but in Fochville the positioning of the cameras was such that Danny Becker and I, the on-field umpires, could not rule on anything we didn't see ourselves.

In the next match in Benoni, where Easterns played Natal, gremlins again ruined the show. Karl Hurter, the third umpire, was seated in a shed next to the scoreboard. When Natal's Keith Forde was caught behind by Easterns wicketkeeper Ivan Pistorius after apparently nicking the ball, Hurter was unable to make a decision. Although the camera seemed to indicate a definite nick, there was no sound to help the third umpire make up his mind. Just a week before, Brian Basson, South Africa's director of umpiring, had predicted that batsmen would 'walk' if they knew they'd touched the ball instead of waiting for a TV replay to prove that they had tried to cheat. But that's not how it happened then, nor is it how it happens today. With no sound at his disposal, Hurter rightly declined to give the decision.

When the Proteas played England in December 1999, the local technology of the SABC let us down again. In Port Elizabeth, England's Chris Adams claimed a catch from Jacques Kallis off Phil Tufnell at a stage when the hosts were rebuilding their innings. As the umpire at the bowler's end, I was unsighted. SkyTV, which had the ultra 'slow-mo' camera process, indicated a fair catch. But TV umpire Dave Orchard had only the inconclusive evidence from the SABC on his monitor, which gave the unfair impression that Adams had 'cheated' by claiming a catch.

Other questionable decisions followed in the match, and I admit that I, too, had my bad moments. Be that as it may, the TV replays once again highlighted the old problem of cheating. At the time, former England coach David Lloyd and former England players Peter Willey and Jonathan Agnew were in agreement on the fact that, by being dishonest, players were simply cheating each other. I told a reporter, 'I can make a decision and the batsman will walk off and shake his head, and then you see it on TV. Although he [might have] just missed the ball, you never know. You can only rely on his honesty.'

By 2002, the ICC was looking into extending the role of television umpires to include more than just lbw decisions. The new approach would be put to the test during the Challenge Trophy in Sri Lanka, where I was also to officiate. ICC cricket manager Dave Richardson explained that the trial would allow umpires to consult TV replays on almost any decision, but that there was a long list of guidelines stipulating when umpires should perhaps *not* consult the replays.

'In nine out of 10 cases, we expect umpires to make up their own minds about whether batsmen are out or not,' Richardson said. The ICC was also trying to gauge how many replays a television umpire should be allowed to have; in some cases they could decide that two replays were too few, in others to limit them to two. And the new lbw guidelines allowed umpires, in certain cases, to check on the height at which a ball had hit the pad.

Television would also assist in caught-behind decisions, with the third umpire looking at a slow-motion replay from both the front and from behind. The main aims of the ICC were to establish whether the use of cameras led to better decision-making, whether the additional use of cameras caused undue delays, and whether the extended role of TV cameras simply confused umpires and players. Despite all this, umpires were still expected to make the majority of the decisions on their own – they could not simply hand the difficult decisions over to the television umpire so that they would be absolved from making mistakes.

At the time, I was one of two South African representatives on the ICC Elite Panel of Umpires. Although I welcomed the innovations, I did suggest that any umpire who was guilty of abusing the situation should be thrown off the panel. We were on the panel because we were the so-called best umpires in the game, and therefore should never be guilty of taking the easy option by referring every decision to the TV umpire. I certainly wanted to make most of my own decisions, but if I had huge doubt in my mind, I was glad to know the decision could be made by a referral.

I also welcomed the extended role of television replays, which would show when players were blatantly cheating. There are many times when a bowler will appeal while knowing full well that a batsman is not out. I was hoping that the replays would expose bowlers who cheated in this way and that, as a result, the crazy appeals would stop.

So, in September 2002, during the Challenge Trophy between Sri Lanka and Pakistan in Colombo, I became the first TV umpire to whom an lbw decision was referred. Pakistan batsman Shoaib Malik was rapped on the pads by Chaminda Vaas, and Daryl Harper, not convinced by the lbw appeal, referred the decision upstairs, to me. After watching the replay, I could confirm the lbw. Daryl said afterwards that he would have given the batsman the benefit of the doubt, so it just goes to show.

During the ICC Champions Trophy in September 2004, the experiment was extended so that the third umpire could call no-balls, which gave on-field umpires more time to watch the ball in flight. But the third umpire found the task of watching two monitors, focused on the popping crease, to be a lot more difficult than imagined.

In October 2004, the matches between Australia and the World XI served as a trial for on-field umpires to refer *all* decisions, barring catches close to the ground, to the television umpire. Aleem Dar and Simon Taufel were appointed as on-field umpires for the first ODI at the Telstra Dome in Melbourne, and I was the television umpire. For the Test, I would be on-field, with Darrell Hair in the stands.

According to the trial guidelines, decisions that involved nicks, the line and height of the ball in lbw appeals, and no-balls could be referred to the third umpire. In principle it meant that every dismissal, including bowled and clear catches, could be referred. In the case of lbws, umpires could ask not only for a ruling on where the ball had pitched, but also obtain valuable feedback to determine the height of the ball and whether there had been a nick. The third umpire, however, had to base his decisions only on the television replays; he could not consult Hawk-Eye. Also, he still did not have the power to reverse an incorrect decision or give unsolicited advice.

After the tournament, the overall view seemed to be that either the system needed more fine-tuning or things should be left as they were, although a minority did welcome the innovation. I, for one, made it clear that I was against the extended use of referrals that included catches and leg-before decisions. 'We all make mistakes, and I think the players actually make more mistakes than the umpires do,' I told a reporter. 'So they should leave it up to us to make the mistakes. We've got to live with that ... Who knows how far they're going to take it?'

Simon Taufel pointed out that the innovation had added to instead of reduced the number of decision-making processes – deciding whether or not to use the third umpire. He also bemoaned the fact that the many stoppages inhibited the momentum of the game. 'It's nice to have it,' Taufel said, 'but I'm just trying to umpire normally, as though the technology isn't there. If I've got no idea about what took place, the help is obviously there.'

Some of us also believed that the increasing use of technology would breed mediocrity among officials, as they would more often than not go for the soft option instead of making unpopular decisions.

Ricky Ponting felt the technology had to be tested a lot more before anyone could get a really good grip on the way it should be used. He pointed out that everyone had thought that by using technology every decision would be perfect, but that the subtleties in some dismissals had been hard to pick up. World XI captain Graeme Smith had similar reservations. He said there were instances where the players thought a batsman was out and he was given not out, or that the batsman was not out and he was given out. 'You try to take the human element out of the [on-field] umpires,' he said, 'but you are still giving [the decision] to the third umpire, so I think there's a lot of things that need to be looked at with the technology.' Glenn McGrath said umpires were still going to make mistakes despite using technology, and suggested that it only be used for stumpings and run-outs.

During the Super Test there were 21 referrals: five for run-outs/ stumpings, 11 for catches and lbw decisions, and five for boundary decisions. The average delay was one minute. On the first day, Australian batsmen were given out three times by the third umpire after the decision was referred. Later on it emerged that some of the appeals that had been referred were barely made clearer by the television replays. In the first innings I gave Mark Boucher out caught behind off Shane Warne, and Inzamam-ul-Haq lbw to Brett Lee in the second innings, but others felt I should have referred these decisions to third umpire Darrell Hair.

ICC chief executive Malcolm Speed stressed that the tournament had served only as a trial – the first time a trial had taken place in a Test match – but he also pointed out that 'we have seen a number of referrals from the two best umpires in the world over the course of the game, and that should tell you something'. What we did realise was that while almost everyone had thought that every decision was going to be perfect because of the help of technology, it wasn't that simple, as many incidents were no clearer on television.

Prior to the 2006/07 Ashes (held Down Under), Australia made an interesting suggestion: that umpires from both nations be allowed to officiate in the series. However, England skipper Andrew Strauss said he was happy with the system as it was and saw no reason to change it. The England Cricket Board supported Strauss by saying that they were comfortable with the ICC's well-established system of using neutral umpires.

In May 2008 the ICC decided on introducing a television referral system, similar to the one used in tennis. Captains and players would now be allowed to challenge umpiring decisions if they disagreed with a call. Each team was given three referrals per innings, and if a decision was successfully challenged, the quota of three referrals remained intact.

The trial was supposed to have taken place in England, but the England players opposed it, and instead it was tried in the Sri Lanka/India series in Sri Lanka later in 2008. In this series, the third umpire's role itself underwent a significant change, as a TV technology trial umpire was introduced in addition to the customary third umpire. I was appointed in this new role, and had the Hawk-Eye at my disposal to assist me in making decisions. (Of course, the Hawk-Eye's predictive element still depended on the individual who operated it.) Along with Asoka de Silva as third umpire, I was to rule on stumpings, run-outs and any other TV decisions.

The two captains for the series, Kumble and Jayawardene, welcomed the new trial, as they believed the technology would eliminate any obvious mistakes. However, they did not see the trial as an opportunity to question every decision the umpire made. As Kumble said, sometimes, in the heat of the moment, the umpires 'might not have picked up an edge during an lbw appeal and they give you out, and those kinds of moments probably will be sorted out, as [they] might change the course of the game'.

But it wasn't all that simple. In the first Test, Harbhajan Singh's vociferous appeal for a leg-before made Kumble wonder whether he should take a chance and refer it, despite the fact that Singh had been bowling around the wicket and India had only two reviews left. Kumble finally decided to ask for the review, but the first replay showed that the ball had pitched a couple of inches outside the line of leg stump, and the batsman could not be given out. That meant India had only one wild card left with another six wickets to get.

Virender Sehwag became the first batsman to be given out by the third umpire under the new referral system. He padded up to a ball from Muralitharan, who was bowling around the wicket, and which pitched on leg. Umpire Mark Benson turned down the appeal, but the Sri Lankans asked for the review. Jayawardene had previously said that if the wicketkeeper and the bowler were not 100 per cent sure that they were right, they would not ask for a review, but this time they did. Looking at the replay, I saw the ball deflecting off the front pad in line with leg stump onto the back pad, plumb in front of middle. I conferred with Benson, and he reversed his decision. Sehwag had to walk.

In another instance, Dilshan was on one run when Zaheer Khan bowled one across his bat. There was a big plume of dust as well as a sound, and Benson thought for a moment and then gave Dilshan out. But Dilshan stood his ground, and Benson signalled me for the replay. The Snickometer wasn't in use at the time, as its efficacy was still in doubt, while Hot Spot had not yet been officially tested for accuracy. In the end, I couldn't be sure whether the sound had been made by a thin edge or the bat striking the turf. I told Benson so and he had little option but to change his decision. Ironically, before the Test, ICC general manager Dave Richardson had emphasised to the media that the final decision would be made by the on-field umpire!

Later in the game, Billy Doctrove and Benson turned down appeals for caught against Tendulkar and Dravid, but replays showed that they did get bat to ball and they were given out. The Sri Lankans could not have afforded to let these two guys have second lives, so here the system did prove its worth.

In the second Test I stood on-field with Mark Benson, with Billy Doctrove upstairs. After the Test, Benson said that the system needed the Hot Spot, and that in the case of lbws, the review should check if the entire ball had pitched outside the line of leg stump instead of working on percentages – at the time, the rule required that more than 50 per cent of the ball had to be pitched in line with leg stump.

Television replays were also used during the Stanford Super Series, which concluded with the US$20 million Stanford Twenty20 match between England and the Stanford Superstars. It was the biggest prize on offer in the game at that stage. Simon Taufel, Asad Rauf, Steve Davis and I were the umpires.

In December 2008 the review system was further trialled in the Test series between New Zealand and the West Indies, but in this instance both captains were concerned about the use of the review system, as the technology available to the third umpire was limited to normal TV coverage. Brendon McCullum's dismissal on the last day of the second Test was a case in point. I gave him out caught behind, but the decision was referred. It was then upheld by third umpire Mark Benson, who had to make the call with only normal TV coverage at his disposal. The more advanced Hot Spot, however, showed no contact between bat and ball.

Afterwards, Kiwi captain Daniel Vettori asked that all available technology be used under the review system to avoid making similar mistakes. He said that it had been obvious that McCullum didn't get a touch to the ball, and that when referrals are made, a third umpire should have access to as much technology as possible. In his opinion, a combination of the Hot Spot, the Snickometer and the naked eye would ensure that the correct decision was made 100 per cent of the time.

The England/West Indies series in early February 2009 in Jamaica was the third to trial the review system. By then the ICC had already tweaked it a bit, reducing the number of reviews available to each team from three to two per innings. Tony Hill and I were the on-field umpires in the first Test at Sabina Park. Devon Smith was given out lbw to Andrew Flintoff after Hill had originally turned down the appeal, while Ramnaresh Sarwan was reprieved after Hill had given a decision in Steve Harmison's favour. Five decisions were reviewed during the second day's play, all in the space of 12 overs. One of the issues that again raised its head was the time it took to make the decisions.

The following month, when Steve Bucknor stood in his last outing as umpire before retiring from Test cricket in the third Test between South Africa and Australia in Cape Town, he asked that the decision-making be left to the on-field officials. It was Bucknor's 128th Test, and this would be the first time he was involved in the player referral system. Although he had no qualms about experimenting with the system, he felt that the standing umpires, and not the players, should send decisions upstairs for review.

'I have nothing against the experiments,' he said, 'but [umpires] know when the decisions are tight. And rather than having a team not capitalising because they have used all their referrals, I hope that later on it [will] be the umpires asking [for a review] rather than the players.'

When I stood in my 100th Test in the Ashes series at Lord's in July 2009, a lot of controversy surrounded some of the dismissals. Once again, I was disappointed by the attitude of batsmen who refuse to walk when they know they've nicked the ball. It's a shame the way they go about it. A batsman will nick the ball, then stand there and wait for the umpires to make the decision. To me, that's nothing but cheating. I don't know why they don't just walk off the park and make it easy for the game. Now wouldn't that be a pleasure? Similarly, I don't like it when fielders claim catches when they're not sure they were catches. Players know that they can cheat and get away with it, and they will try their luck. Sometimes it works, sometimes it doesn't. But why do it at all? Cricket is supposed to be a gentleman's game.

At Lord's, I was standing with Billy Doctrove. When we referred Nathan Hauritz's claimed catch of Ravi Bopara to the TV umpire but not Andrew Strauss's claimed catch of Australian opener Philip Hughes, we were heavily criticised for our supposed inconsistency. In the Hauritz incident, I saw the batsman play a shot, and for a moment or so I lost sight of the ball; all I saw next was Hauritz's hands going down. I wasn't sure whether or not he had caught the ball, so I asked Billy Doctrove. 'I'm not sure either, Rudi,' he said. 'I missed the flight of the ball.' So what can we do but refer the matter upstairs? After all, that's what the rule requires. To the third umpire, it was inconclusive; he doesn't see things in 3D.

As for the Strauss incident, I couldn't see where the catch was taken because the bowler was running down the wicket. As I didn't have a clue, I walked over to Billy and asked him if it had been a fair catch. 'Yes,' he said, 'it went straight in.' The rule says that as long as one of the on-field umpires is sure the ball has carried, the decision stays on-field.

Ricky Ponting's first-innings dismissal made me even more unpopular with Australian fans. I heard two sounds, as if he had nicked the ball, but I wasn't sure whether the ball had carried to Strauss at slip. So I asked the third umpire to determine if the ball had carried. He confirmed that it had, and I gave Ponting the slow death. Replays, which I didn't see, suggested the ball had hit Ponting's foot and not the bat. But I had definitely heard two sounds, and if he hadn't touched the ball, I would have given him out lbw anyway. But the catch had come first, which is why I'd gone upstairs to see if the ball had carried. The noises were perfect for bat on ball and I gave Ponting out. I was later told that when they put the magnifier on the ball, it showed it had missed the bat. If I'd made the wrong decision, I'll put up my hand and say, 'Sorry, I cocked it up.'

Hopefully the introduction of the decision review system – which had been on trial in the four series mentioned – will go a long way towards eliminating the kind of controversies described above. I certainly hope it will help us to get the bad decisions we sometimes make, right. Ironically, many top Australian players had been against the referral system when it was trialled in the Test series in South Africa, but perhaps now they will change their minds. The system was phased in from October 2009, and Australia used it in their home Test series against the West Indies and Pakistan.

I've been in meetings where Ponting said, 'Let's try it' – that is, accept the umpire's word – but then you get to the second day in a Test match and someone claims a catch and 10 minutes later you hear, 'The ball didn't carry,' and the argument starts all over again. I say, let's use the technology if it's available.

I've been involved in three of the four video-review series and the system was definitely helpful. But the technology should be spot-on. A TV umpire has to be sure of his decision – he can't just guess and 15 minutes later the producers find another angle that shows he made the wrong decision. Hot Spot is a very good innovation, but I'm not sure whether Hawk-Eye is absolutely accurate. Yet the third umpire should have access to every bit of technology available. I believe it can improve our decision-making from the present 98 per cent to about 99 per cent, with the ultimate aim being to obtain a 100 per cent success rate so that we can eliminate the crucial decisions we get wrong at the wrong time from the game.

Of course it is true that some umpires jealously protect the power they have over the players (and I'm talking cricket at all levels here) and see the use of technology as a threat to their authority. Then there are those who suggest that third umpires are reluctant to overrule their fellow umpires out in the middle when players appeal against a decision. But I think most of the players see the technological innovations as a positive development and not as an attempt to undermine umpires' decisions. Will there be captains who won't refer a decision because they are reluctant to offend an umpire who might officiate in their future matches? I don't think so.

By the end of 2009, the CEO of the ICC, David Richardson, could report that the DRS has improved the percentage of correct decisions from 93 per cent to 98 per cent. That may not sound like much, but in the greater scheme of things, it is a significant percentage. If the system has helped to eliminate an absolute howler here and there, then it has been fulfilling its purpose.

While I was standing in Australia, South Africa and England battled it out in South Africa to draw their series 1-all, and, from what I read in the media, referrals were again a big talking point. In the fourth and final Test at the Wanderers, England coach Andy Flower was furious after South African captain Graeme Smith survived a controversial decision review. Smith (who eventually scored 105) was on 15 when he flashed at a wide delivery from Ryan Sidebottom, and the fielders were convinced he had edged the ball to wicketkeeper Matt Prior. When umpire Tony Hill turned down the appeal, England asked for the review, but third umpire Daryl Harper then upheld Hill's decision. Flower said Harper had erred by not turning up the volume on his feed from the stump microphone, and that the England camp could clearly hear an edge on their TV sets in the changing room. 'If the incident had not happened in such a serious match I would have found it amusing,' Flower said. 'But it is very disappointing and incidents like these do not reflect well on the ICC.'

Flower said that, despite the fact that Dave Richardson and Roshan Mahanama (the match referee) had said before the start of the series that an increased volume would be used on the stump microphones in the absence of a Snickometer and the Hot Spot, the volume had apparently been turned down on the third umpire's feed. Mahanama explained afterwards that TV umpires receive sound feeds at a different level to that which others are receiving, as various broadcasters use different technologies while televising – as was the case in Johannesburg.

Graeme Smith acknowledged that there had been a sound, but he could neither confirm nor deny that his bat had touched the ball. I don't know about that. No matter at what level you're playing, whether in a village cricket game or in a Test, I say a batsman knows only too well when he's nicked the ball, however faint it may be. If Smith did get a touch, he should have walked. Flower also bemoaned the fact that the system is not used for no-balls, and that both Kevin Pietersen and Graeme Smith had been dismissed off no-balls in the series.

South African coach Mickey Arthur added his penny's worth to the controversy. Writing in *The Wisden Cricketer* magazine, Arthur said: 'I was always in favour of the DRS, but now that we have seen the system in operation for a decent period of time, I have mixed feelings. Incorrect umpiring decisions can affect the results of matches and also players' careers, so I felt that anything that could bring more correct decisions had to be good for the game. The system is definitely more good than bad, but I do have some misgivings. We have to standardise the use of the DRS across the world by using all the tools available. If Hot Spot and Snicko are used in one series but not another, then the system is half-baked.' I fully agree that if we're going to use all the technology, there should be consistency.

Arthur said he was not 100 per cent convinced about the pre-dictive element of Hawk-Eye – and he won't be the last to say that – and neither were many of the players. The other issue that needs to be clarified, he said, is the amount of time taken to decide whether to call for a review. In Australia it was 10 seconds, but in the South Africa/England series, players were given 25 seconds. Interestingly, Arthur anticipated more lbws given under the DRS on the Proteas upcoming tour of India, 'because height and bounce are rarely an issue'.

It is going to be a big challenge for umpires to get used to the new system. Are they just going to stand out in the middle and use television whenever they can, or will they go out there and still do what they're used to doing? Umpires will have to accept that any mistakes they make will be rectified, which they have to be big enough to handle. The point is surely that the right decision will be made, which is what umpires want, after all. It's a good thing we have technology, especially with all the big money in the sport today. I remember the days when the word of the fielder was good enough. Now, no one is walking.

I was once asked if I knew immediately when I'd made a mistake. Yes, I know when I've made a mistake. As soon as the batsman walks off the field, I can see from his body language whether or not I have got it wrong. I want the right decision to be made. If a player challenges a decision I've made and it turns out I was wrong, I am happy to reverse the call. To me, the most important thing in my career is having the players' respect, and I would like to respect them in return.

12

The best of the best

" *But for sheer batting brutality, no one can emulate Adam Gilchrist. His 204 against South Africa at the Wanderers in 2002 was the most ruthless display of stroke play I've seen in my time. Whether he opened the batting or went in at no. 7, whether it was a Test or an ODI, Gilchrist always went after the bowling.* "

During my more than two decades of umpiring, I have had the honour of seeing the world's top players from up close in various corners of the globe. I made my first-class umpiring debut in the 1980s and have been standing in Tests and ODIs since 1992, and in that time I have seen many promising youngsters fall by the wayside – but I have also seen the wonderful talent of yesterday develop into the top stars who are gracing the world's cricket fields today. I would like to share with you my thoughts on those players I have most enjoyed watching. In order to best depict their abilities as batsmen or bowlers, I have inevitably had to quote some basic statistics here and there.

It is probably unfair of me to single out only two players, but I would rate Sachin Tendulkar and Brian Lara as the best batsmen I've seen in all my umpiring years. Their amazing reflexes allowed them to pick up the ball as soon as it left the bowler's hand. With their superb timing, excellent footwork and ability to find the gaps, they made batting look graceful and elegant, and they could score runs even off good balls. At least Sachin will still be around for a while, but it was sad to see Brian retire in 2007. They're not the kind of batsmen you can replace overnight. Their kind only comes around every few decades, and I count myself very fortunate to have seen them when they were at their brilliant best.

Tendulkar's success can be attributed to his tremendous ability to focus – one is almost surprised that his highest score is only 248 not out! He has perfect balance, excellent anticipation and a full range of shots; when he wants to, he can improvise as well. He was only 17 when he scored his first Test century, and in 271 Test innings he has scored 47 hundreds and 54 fifties at an average of 55.56, and another 46 hundreds and 93 fifties in 431 ODI innings. That is tremendous stuff. On top of this, in February 2010 he became the first man in history to score a double century in an ODI (against South Africa in Gwalior).

Interestingly, when Sachin was once asked which bowlers had troubled him the most, he named Pedro Collins and Hansie Cronjé. He was also quoted as saying, 'I once told my partner, "Will you please take Hansie for me? I don't mind playing Allan Donald."' Sachin is not a shabby bowler himself. He has taken 44 wickets in Tests, with best figures of 3/10.

Just to show that Sachin is human after all, referee Mike Denness found him guilty of ball tampering in 2001 at St George's Park in Port Elizabeth. He was banned for one Test match, with the sentence suspended until the end of the year, and fined 75 per cent of his match fee – which would have been quite a bit of money.

Brian Lara was 'already' 20 years old when he made his Test debut, compared to Tendulkar, who was 16 on Test debut. Since then no one since the great Donald Bradman made big scores as often and as quickly as Lara. Within two months in 1994, his 375 and 501 not out set new world records for the highest Test and first-class scores. In Sri Lanka in 2001/02 he scored 688 runs in the Test series, with a record 42 per cent of the West Indies' total in runs; later, in Antigua, when England toured the West Indies, he scored an unbeaten 400 in the last Test. At times, the captaincy of a side notorious for their indiscipline must have weighed heavily on his shoulders, but at least he'd led the one-day team to the title in the ICC Champions Trophy. In 2006, he also skippered the West Indies to a 4-1 ODI series victory over India.

Lara bowed out on his home soil during the 2007 World Cup, a sad moment for cricket fans all around the world. In 232 Test innings, he'd scored almost 12 000 runs, with a highest score of 400 not out and an average of almost 53. He scored 34 hundreds and 48 fifties in Tests, and also boasted an ODI average of just over 40, with 19 centuries and 63 fifties. When he retired, he had a total of 65 first-class hundreds behind his name.

A man I saw in action often during my Test-umpiring career and admired for his batting was Australia's Steve Waugh. He played to his strengths, minimising any risks and waiting patiently for the loose ball – and he could punish it severely. In 260 Test innings, he scored almost 11 000 runs, averaging 51, with a highest score of 200, which he scored in Jamaica in the 1994/95 season. Waugh scored 32 hundreds and 50 fifties in Tests, and another three hundreds and 45 fifties in ODIs.

I admired him greatly as a captain, and he was one of the most successful in the game. He led Australia in 15 of their world-record 16 successive Test victories, to the 1999 World Cup title and another Ashes trophy in 2002/03, before retiring at the end of the 2003/04 series against India.

Over the years, I also saw a lot of former Australian opener Matthew Hayden. Evidence that once he got his nose past 50 he more often than not went all the way to a hundred lies in the remarkable fact that he'd scored more Test hundreds (30) than fifties (29). His big opening partnerships with Justin Langer were always a joy to watch. In 184 Test innings, he averaged 50, with a highest score of 380 runs. His ODI average was almost 44, with 10 centuries and 36 fifties, and he had a highest score of 181. In addition he was an outstanding catcher in the slips and gully.

Hayden's success lay in the fact that he had both mental and physical strength. Tall and powerful, he had excellent concentration and could smash the ball through the off-side all day long. In India in 2000/01 he scored 549 runs, an Australian record for a three-Test series, and by mid-2004 he had taken his tally to 20 centuries in only 55 Tests. He became only the third player next to Donald Bradman and Ken Barrington to score four hundreds in a row twice. In the Chappell-Hadlee ODI series, he made a record 181 runs off 166 balls, which included 10 sixes, and at the 2007 World Cup he averaged 73 in scoring 659 runs, the most at the tournament. In St Kitts, at the World Cup, he smashed a brutal hundred off only 66 balls against South Africa. Hayden was another favourite whom I was sorry to see retire at the beginning of 2009.

This brings me to arguably the most prolific Australian run-scorer of all time. Not everybody's cup of tea, but what a player! Ricky Ponting has rewritten his country's batting record books with 39 hundreds and 49 fifties at an amazing average of almost 56 per innings and a highest score of 257. He has already knocked up more than 11 000 runs. In ODIs he has scored more than 12 000 runs, with 28 hundreds and 73 fifties, averaging 43. In Twenty20, his highest score is an unbeaten 98. He can be very intense on the field, as one can understand from an international captain, and he has been found guilty a few times for poor on-field behaviour.

Ponting has enjoyed a large measure of success as skipper after succeeding Steve Waugh, leading Australia to the 2003 World Cup title and scoring 140 not out in the final. In 2007, he led the Aussies to a third consecutive World Cup win, his second as captain. In 2006, he led the 5-0 demolition of England to regain the Ashes, earning the Man of the Series award with 576 runs at an average of 82.28. Only Tendulkar has more centuries to his name than Ponting.

I have also enjoyed watching Sri Lanka's Mahela Jayawardene, who appeared on the Test scene in 1997. Technically he is out-standing, and his great temperament has enabled him to bat for long periods of time and make the big scores. He was playing in only his seventh Test when he scored a double century, and he still holds the record for a Sri Lankan batsman with 374 runs, a record he took from another master at the crease, Sanath Jayasuriya. He scored that big innings against South Africa at the SSC in Colombo in 2006, establishing a new first-class third-wicket part-nership with Sangakkara of 624 runs.

Jayawardene has scored the most Test hundreds for his country, 26 in 177 innings, as well as 35 fifties, at an outstanding average of 53. His ODI form is not as great, but is nevertheless still quite good, with 11 hundreds in 291 innings, averaging 32 and with a highest score of 128.

He also proved to be a very capable skipper, and in 2006 led Sri Lanka to a 5-0 whitewash over England after injury ruled out Marvan Atapattu. I was umpiring on-field at Lord's when he showed his fine temperament again to score a fighting 119 as Sri Lanka pulled off an amazing rearguard action to save the match. As one-day captain he led Sri Lanka to the final of the 2007 World Cup. Early in 2009, however, he resigned as captain after Sri Lanka was defeated 1-4 in the home ODI series against India.

But for sheer batting brutality, no one can emulate Adam Gilchrist. His 204 against South Africa at the Wanderers in 2002 was the most ruthless display of stroke play I've seen in my time. Whether he opened the batting or went in at no. 7, whether it was a Test or an ODI, Gilchrist always went after the bowling and was arguably the most exhilarating cricketer of the modern era. Gillie was the ultimate team man; he only cared for his side's score on the board and never for his own average. An easy-going, country-boy type, he brought something special to the game. I once gave him not out in a World Cup match after he had nicked the ball, but he walked anyway – a rarity among players these days.

Years from now I will still be able to picture him clearly, his hands high on the bat's handle, whacking good balls through gaps and way over the ropes. In Tests he scored at 81 runs per 100 balls, and in ODIs at 96 runs per 100 balls, and he averaged 46. His 17 hundreds and 26 fifties in Tests included no fewer than 100 sixes. His highest Test score was the 204 I mentioned at first; in ODIs it was 172. One of his most memorable innings came in the 2007 World Cup final against Sri Lanka, when he scored 149 runs off just 104 balls, slamming 13 fours and eight sixes in the process. Apart from his spectacular 204 at the Wanderers, he smashed a remarkable century off 57 deliveries in the Ashes Test in Perth. What a pleasure to have a wicketkeeper of such batting ability! And as a keeper, he snatched 379 catches in Tests and stumped 37; in ODIs his stats read 417 catches and 55 stumpings.

Gilchrist also made his mark as Australian Test captain, leading Australia to their first series win in India in 35 years (2004/05).

When it came to power hitting, few could match the Kiwi Chris Cairns, one of the more colourful characters in the game. His career stats show that in 104 Test innings, he only scored five centuries, but that he hit no fewer than 86 sixes and 365 fours; in 193 ODI innings, he scored four centuries, hit 345 fours and 153 sixes. That's a lot of balls that have gone all the way. He wasn't a bad bowler either, with best bowling figures of 7/27 in a Test innings and an average economy rate of just over three per over. In his time, he became only the sixth man to achieve an all-rounder's double of 200 wickets and 3 000 runs.

Chris Gayle is another one of those players who seems to hit the ball for miles with minimum effort. He's not a man with much footwork at the crease, like a Lara or a Tendulkar. Tall and imposing, this son of Jamaica is one of the most laid-back batsmen at the crease I've ever come across, and he shows scant respect no matter who is bowling at him. I saw him slam a hundred off just 79 balls in Cape Town in 2004, and it's the one innings for which I will always remember him.

Since his debut in 2000, Gayle has scored 10 Test centuries, but one would have expected more. His 317 against South Africa in Antigua showed that he also has the temperament to go well beyond the 100 mark. In 144 Test innings, Gayle has hit 837 fours. Like few others, he can hit the ball through the covers off either the front or the back foot – and how spectacularly well does he do it! Like Cairns, he can bowl a bit of off-spin, too, sporting best Test-innings figures of 5/34. Usually a placid fellow, he was quite animated in the 2006 ICC Champions Trophy when Michael Clarke allegedly told the West Indian that he was a 'second-class citizen'. Gayle was fined 30 per cent of his match fee, but Clarke was found not guilty. Clarke's reply was that 'if anyone is second-class it's me. I'm from Liverpool' (a working-class suburb in Sydney).

As far as big hitters go, the two England batsmen Kevin Pietersen and Andrew Flintoff often brightened up my day. Kevin, of course, is South African–born, but he is not the most popular guy in the country when he visits South Africa. I really don't know why people hold it against him for choosing to follow a career in England when he was obviously going nowhere in South Africa. I wonder how many of his critics have kids who are working in England right now!

I first saw Kevin when he played for Natal as essentially an off-break spinner, before he opted to go and play county cricket for Nottinghamshire and Hampshire. There's a world of difference between what he was then and what he has now become. In his first year playing for England, Kevin scored three ODI centuries against the Proteas in South Africa, despite the hostile reception he received at the grounds, and a century in the Ashes – the latter I describe in the Ashes chapters. Before the 2009/10 series against South Africa, he boasted a Test average of a fraction under 50 in 97 outings, with 16 hundreds and 15 fifties, and a highest test score of 226 (against the West Indies). In ODIs, his average was 45.

Although Kevin may be too flamboyant for some folks, cricket needs characters, just like any sport does. More importantly, he makes runs for England. He's the kind of guy for whom spectators abandon pubs to go and watch him bat. His cocky confidence may offend some people, but it works for him. Although not exactly the most elegant of batsmen, Kevin has a wonderful eye and can hit a ball damn hard. One can sense that he resents being dominated by any bowler, even a Shane Warne, and he will have a go soon enough to break the shackles. Sometimes it works for him, sometimes it doesn't, but when he does come off, he's exhilarating to watch. No wonder that, along with Andrew Flintoff, he secured the most lucrative IPL contract, said to be worth $1.5 million a year.

Of the South African players I have seen since the country's readmission to international cricket, Jacques Kallis has been the one who stood out. While he has a wide array of attacking shots, Jacques is more efficient than he is spectacular, and his averages of 54 in Tests and 45 in ODIs are testimony to his consistency. He always seems to be guarding his wicket with his life, and bowlers know they have to work very hard for it.

So far Jacques has 33 Test centuries behind his name, but his value to the Proteas has been as much for his all-round ability. He has already taken 260 wickets in Tests at an economy rate of under three per over, with a best performance of 6/54. In ODIs, he has taken 248 wickets with a best of 5/30. There's no doubt that until Andrew Flintoff appeared on the scene, Jacques was the leading all-rounder in the world. At the 2007 World Cup, he was the Proteas' highest run-scorer, with 485. He wasn't the ICC Test Player of the Year in 2005 for nothing.

Speaking of Flintoff, I, for one, was disappointed to see big Freddie retire from international cricket in July 2009. He had surely been England's best all-rounder since Ian Botham. Whether he played for England or the Chennai Super Kings, he was a devastating hitter of the ball who could quickly turn a game on its head. As a bowler, he had genuine pace, with tricky reverse-swing. Unfortunately he was plagued by back and ankle injuries and at times struggled with his weight. I would say Freddie reached his greatest heights in the 2005 Ashes, in which I was fortunate to umpire, scoring around 400 runs and taking 24 wickets. Freddie loves a good party, which was why I was a bit taken aback when he was appointed England skipper in 2006. As it turned out, his captaincy didn't last very long.

I think he was a better player than his five centuries and 26 fifties in Tests, and an average of around 31, suggest. He had a better average in ODIs – 32 – with three hundreds and 18 fifties behind his name. His reputation as a big hitter is clearly reflected in his stats for both Test and ODI cricket. In 130 Test innings, he blasted no fewer than 82 sixes and 513 fours, and another 93 sixes and 308 fours in 122 ODI innings. As a bowler, he boasted best innings figures of 5/58 and best match figures of 8/156.

Speaking of genuine all-rounders, South African Clive Rice was one of a few fantastic players whom I did not see in action in Tests because of South Africa's isolation years, but I saw plenty of him while umpiring in South Africa's domestic competition during the 1980s and early 1990s. I have no doubt that had he had the chance of playing official Tests and ODIs, he would have made his mark as one of the world's great all-rounders. Sadly, he only featured in three official ODIs for South Africa, and that when his career was already coming to an end.

A more competitive player and captain than Rice you could not have found, and he was the driving force behind the Transvaal 'Mean Machine' of the 1970s and 1980s. At the same time he was a key figure in Nottinghamshire's success on the English county circuit. Clive could hit the ball very hard, his trademark a savage cut-shot, and as a bowler he generated genuine pace.

During the 1980s he was an automatic choice for South Africa against the several international rebel touring teams that visited the country. He was a no-nonsense captain and, like Hansie and Kepler, led from the front in terms of commitment in an era when the guys were a lot more relaxed about fielding practice and fitness than today.

A never-say-die player, Clive will be remembered for his stunning bowling performance in the 1980s against Kim Hughes's rebel Australians in Port Elizabeth. The Aussies needed only 18 runs to win and had eight wickets in hand, and it should have been a formality. But, typically, Clive never gave up, and he ripped through the Australian line-up to win the match for South Africa.

His stats speak for themselves. In a first-class career that ranged from the 1969/70 to the 1993/94 season, Clive batted in 482 innings and averaged 40, with 48 centuries and 137 fifties. At the same time, he took 930 wickets, with best figures of 7/62.

Now let's get to the bowlers. Yes, you've guessed it. There's not been anyone like Australian leg spinner Shane Warne. Being an umpire when the great Warne was at your end was something special, and while the batsmen were relieved, I was really sorry to see one of the most charismatic and flamboyant of players retire from Test cricket after Australia's whitewash of England in 2006/07.

I have always admired fast bowlers like Glenn McGrath and Allan Donald, but the bowler who stands out for me is Shane Warne. He used to get the best out of the umpires by putting a lot of pressure on them. On numerous occasions he bowled from my end, and I always found him testing my decision-making. You had to concentrate extremely hard when he was bowling because he had so much variety and variation that every ball he bowled was potentially a wicket-taking delivery. Shane could spin a ball, all right, and he was right on the money from the word go; with it, he had this rare ability to impose his will on any given occasion.

Some people found him arrogant, which may have been because he didn't lack any self-confidence, but off the field he was a really nice guy and would always find the time to come and chat. On the field, he underwent a personality change. He was hard and competitive and when things didn't go his way, he'd get grumpy. You couldn't just shake your head when you denied him a decision and think that was that. Shane always wanted to know *why* not. With him you had to keep your back stiff, or he'd make you crack. I once had 38 overs of Warnie from my side of the wicket and, boy, did I know I'd been umpiring Shane Warne's bowling!

To say that he was a mischievous bloke is maybe an understatement, and many newspaper headlines in which he featured had nothing to do with his performances on the field. But he survived it all; in 2000, already, he was rated among the five greatest cricketers of the 20th century, and by 2006 he was bowling better than ever. Speak of Warne and people will remind you of *that* ball that bamboozled Mike Gatting in 1993.

Warne just seemed to get better and better as the years went on. In 2004 he removed 26 Sri Lankan batsmen in three Tests, and the following year he claimed a world-record 96 victims, 24 more than in his sensational haul of 1993. Forty of those were from the thrilling Ashes series. He had an amazing variety of balls, relying mostly on his wonderful accuracy and the leg break, but controlling and mixing his degree of spin at will. He also took a Test hat-trick, and was the first cricketer to reach 700 Test wickets. He was also no monkey with the bat, and hit more runs than any other Test player without making a century.

In his 145 Tests, Warne took 708 wickets, with best figures of 8/71 and best match figures of 12/128, with an economy rate of 2.65. He also achieved a five-wicket haul in an innings 37 times. In ODIs, he added 293 wickets, with best figures of 5/33. As a batsman, he scored 3154 runs, with a highest score of 99 – sadly, as mentioned, he never got a hundred – and 12 fifties.

And then there's Muri. Sri Lanka's Muttiah Muralitharan has become the world's leading wicket-taker, averaging almost six wickets per Test, but the cricket world has been divided as a result of his strange bent-arm action and he has become the most controversial cricketer of the modern era. Muri can bowl for long periods at a time, getting turn on any surface, and uses to devastating effect his prodigiously spinning off-break, his top-spinner which goes straight on, and the doosra, spinning in the opposite direction. He has also added his own version of the slider, flicked out of the side of his hand and rushing onto batsmen.

Soon after his debut against Australia in 1993, Muri's bowling action raised suspicion, and while touring Australia in 1995/96 he was called for throwing at Melbourne by Darrell Hair. In the one-day series that followed, he was again called. The ICC cleared him, however, after biomechanical tests at the University of Western Australia and also at the University of Hong Kong concluded that his action created the optical illusion of throwing. But that was not the end of it; he was called again on the 1998/99 tour to Australia, this time by umpire Ross Emerson. Further tests in Perth and England cleared him again.

Then, at the end of a prolific three-match home series against Australia in 2004, match referee Chris Broad reported him again, and more tests followed. This forced the ICC to look into the entire issue of throwing in international cricket, and investigations revealed that many bowlers bend their arms during delivery. I doubt, however, whether Muri's action will ever be free of controversy. In 2007, he became the second player to take 700 Test wickets, and in December that year he passed Shane Warne's record of 708 wickets. He also achieved the double of being the highest wicket-taker in ODIs as well when he passed Wasim Akram's record of 502 wickets in 2009. At the time of writing, Muri stood on 792 wickets in 132 Tests, with a best analysis of 9/51.

Now for the fast boys. I was privileged to be umpiring when Glenn McGrath took his 500th wicket in Test cricket in the 2005

Ashes on the first day at Lord's. To mark the occasion, they brought a pair of special '500 wickets' boots onto the field for the tall man.

'You really dig these shoes, don't you?' I pulled his leg.

'Oh, it was hard work to get to 500 wickets,' he said.

'And how many wickets of those 500 that I have given you were not out?' I asked in jest. Like Warne, Glenn could get real grumpy when a batsman got hold of him.

McGrath was one of the very best fast bowlers I've seen in my time, but he had to overcome injuries in the 2005 Ashes series, which I think were crucial to Australia losing the Ashes. The next summer was disrupted by his wife Jane's illness, but he still made a great comeback, taking a record 26 wickets in the 2007 World Cup.

In total, McGrath claimed 563 wickets in Tests, with a best analysis of 8/24, claiming five wickets or more in an innings 29 times. And he was economical: just under 2.5 runs an over; in ODIs, where he took 381 wickets, it was still under four runs an over. He could bowl an off-stump line and immaculate length all day long, get off-cut and terrific bounce, and he was usually the one to take the opposition team's biggest wicket. I don't think any other bowler got Tendulkar as many times as McGrath. By 2006, he had claimed Tendulkar's extremely valuable scalp 13 times at international level.

McGrath made his debut for Australia in 1993 – just after I started Test umpiring – when he replaced Merv Hughes, so I've come a long way with him, so to speak. He went on to become the greatest Australian fast bowler of his time, beating Courtney Walsh's 519 wickets in the 2005 Super Test to become the leading wicket-taker among fast bowlers. He retired from Tests at his home ground, the SCG, after Australia whitewashed England 5-0 in the 2006/07 Ashes, but was still named Player of the Tournament during Australia's successful 2007 World Cup.

Brett Lee, with more than 300 wickets, is a positive and determined bloke, in spite of recurring injuries. When he was younger he was really quick, bowling consistently above 150 km/h, producing unplayable outswingers or yorkers, or at times well-disguised slower deliveries. And he has a good vocabulary when he's beaten a batsman all ends up. Because he's so fast, his deliveries carry to the boundary so much quicker, but his economy rate is well below four an over.

Lee took 20 wickets in the 2006/07 Ashes, but he missed out on the World Cup because of injury. In his comeback in 2007, Lee was going to be Australia's main man, and he didn't disappoint. He took 16 wickets against Sri Lanka and was Player of the Series; he then took another 24 wickets against India, and after the West Indies series he had added 58 more victims to his name. He has come on well with the bat, too, with five Test fifties and a highest score of 64. In the 2005 Ashes he nearly pulled off a win for Australia with a fighting 43 at Edgbaston, before last man Michael Kasprowicz fell at the final hurdle in a two-run defeat. It was nail-biting stuff and probably the most exciting Test in which I've stood.

Talk about fast bowling, and the West Indians immediately spring to mind. One player who stood out for me was the great Malcolm Marshall, who retired from Test cricket at the time that I started my career as Test umpire, but I saw enough of him when he was playing for Natal in South Africa to rank him among the very best I've come across in my time. He was an intelligent cricketer who possessed tremendous courage and stamina, which made him one of the most competitive players in the history of the game.

Marshall was not as tall as a Courtney Walsh or a Curtley Ambrose, but he could still bowl the most vicious bouncer. He just looked the natural, balanced athlete. Twinkle-toed and with an open delivery action, his bowling arm came over lightning fast and he could swing the ball either way at great pace. He was able to extract from dead pitches a bit more than most top bowlers, and in 1988, on an Old Trafford wicket that was prepared for the spinners, he claimed 7/22.

During Marshall's Test career he took 376 wickets – and this at a time when Tests weren't as prolific as today – with a strike rate of 46 and an average of just under 21. He was certainly among the cream of the crop, and his average of 20.94 is unsurpassed by any bowler who has taken 200 and more Test wickets. Marshall was also no mug with the bat, scoring seven first-class centuries and playing some vital Test innings at No. 8, with a highest Test score of 92 against India in 1983/84. Sadly, he tragically died of cancer at the young age of 41 in 1999.

Two other West Indians who really impressed me were Courtney Walsh and Curtley Ambrose. Walsh was a bit of a freak. He bowled faster for longer than any player I can remember, and he had a durability that enabled him to reach the previously undreamt-of milestone of 519 Test wickets. Walsh made his Test debut in 1984 and only retired in 2001, which is a long spell for any fast bowler. In tandem with Ambrose and Marshall, he was the real workhorse, but around 1993 he was a new-ball man and went on to form one of the great opening partnerships with Ambrose. Between them, they bagged 421 scalps in 49 Tests. That's great bowling indeed.

Walsh was by no means an elegant ballet dancer in his action, but he was very economical, and with his height he could send down some nasty bouncers. It took him 132 Tests to reach 519 wickets, and he recorded best innings figures of 7/37 and best match figures of 13/55. In ODIs he claimed another 227 wickets, and once took an incredible 5/1.

Ambrose claimed 405 wickets in his 98 Tests, with best figures of 8/45, and another 225 wickets in ODIs. Like Walsh, he was very economical, averaging 2.3 runs per over, and was arguably the most lethal pace bowler of his generation. He never said much, which just added to his menacing appearance on the field. In the 1993/94 season, when England was skittled in Trinidad for a mere 46 runs, it was Ambrose who claimed six wickets for 24. The year before, he had an incredible burst of 7/1 against Australia at the WACA in Perth. A very tall man, Ambrose could extract bounce that made the lives of batsmen extremely difficult.

South Africa's Allan Donald wasn't known as White Lightning for nothing. With a classic action and sometimes frightening pace, he contributed a great deal to his country's success in the modern era, becoming the first bowler from South Africa to take 300 Test wickets. Towards the end of his career injuries started to take their toll. Donald retired from Test cricket after the home series against Australia in 2001/02, and from ODIs the next year, after South Africa's tragic exit from the 2003 World Cup. He also had a long spell with Warwickshire, where he excelled as much as at home.

The fact that he was given the role of bowling coach with England in 2007 is testimony to the high regard in which he was held over there. In his 72 Tests, he claimed 330 wickets at an economy rate of 2.83, with best innings figures of 8/71 and best match figures of 12/139. He took five wickets and more 20 times in Tests.

To finish off my praises for the best cricketers of my time, I have to mention Jonty Rhodes. Guys like Herschelle Gibbs, AB de Villiers and Ricky Ponting are all exceptional fielders, but for me there can be only one Jonty. Because I loved fielding myself when playing at club level, I really enjoy sublime pieces of fielding, watching from close up as on-field umpire, and I especially enjoyed Jonty.

Who will ever forget his diving run-out of Inzamam-ul-Haq at the 1992 World Cup? That magnificent piece of fielding surely gained him eternal fame – but that's not where his spectacular feats ended. He was a natural athlete, but he never let that be enough for him; through dedication and a great work ethic he maintained his exceptional standards throughout his career. He was simply magnificent fielding at backward point, where he made numerous stops and pulled off stunning acrobatic catches. Just seeing Jonty standing there, batsmen were too inhibited by his reputation to risk a run.

Jonty is a hell of a nice guy and was a wonderful team man, always clapping his hands between deliveries to egg on his teammates. He inspired many a fellow cricketer simply by example.

13

The highs and lows of umpiring

" *In the 2005 Ashes, when the weather was dicey and Kevin Pietersen scored that 158, Shane Warne came on and started pressuring me, saying things like, 'I have to bowl England out,' as if expecting me to help make that happen!* *"*

So what's it like being an international umpire?

Well, for a start you stand out on the field in the blazing sun or in a chilly breeze for six hours a day, five days in a row, surrounded by thousands of rowdy spectators. You have about 30 cameras tracking you all the time, millions of people watching you in their homes, a dozen or more TV commentators scrutinising and criticising your decisions, and a press box full of people writing about the mistakes you make.

If it sounds like being at the bottom of a pressure cooker, you're right, but that's part and parcel of the game. However, let me say right from the outset that I have always felt very lucky to be part of the greatest sport I know, and I wouldn't change my job for anything in the world.

There is a general perception that umpires lead a glamorous life. Yes, it is true that you are in the limelight a lot of the time – it has been an exciting 17 years in the business, and a journey, I'm sure, that many would envy. Every job has its highs and lows, however, and umpiring is no exception. My job gave me the opportunity to travel extensively (in fact, I have worked in 18 different countries). I met different kinds of people and experienced many cultures – it broadened my horizons tremendously. I rubbed shoulders with the game's top players both on and off the field, and for me to have seen the Tendulkars, Laras and Gilchrists of the cricket world from so close behind the stumps was a wonderful experience.

But umpiring is a very demanding job, bringing with it a lot of pressure both on and off the field: scathing and sometimes unnecessary criticism from the media, a lot of tiring travel and long periods away from home. Fortunately, like in all sport, there's a funny side to it, and a host of interesting and colourful characters cross your path. But there's also unpleasantness and insults and even danger, and here I can mention the bomb incident in Karachi as an example. All things considered, however, the highs outweigh the lows and, as I've said, I wouldn't trade my umpiring job for any other.

When I started umpiring way back in Griqualand West, I didn't think I would get this far. I started as a club umpire and they pushed me through the ranks, and 10 weeks later I handled my first first-class game. Initially it all happened very quickly, and since then it has been a long yet rewarding road. Umpiring gave me the opportunity to give something back to the game that I love so much. When I was picked to be on our Test panel in 1992 when South Africa returned to international cricket, I regarded it as a bonus. When I was appointed to stand in the South Africa/India Test in Port Elizabeth, my home ground of all places, I was thinking, 'I'm doing a Test match here when there are a lot of umpires who have never had that opportunity.'

That was a time when umpires used to umpire for the love of the game, but there's no such thing any more. Nowadays, the first thing people discuss is money. All a modern-day umpire wants to know is, 'How much am I going to be paid?' It's sad that

that is the prevailing attitude; we did it because we loved it. Of course we used to get paid for umpiring in the early days, but you couldn't even buy a beer for the money, so to speak. I recall doing a day game for R75, and I could just afford the cab to the ground and back and that was it.

For me it's never been about the money – yes, we all have to earn money to make a decent living – but about the great honour of being part of the sport. I'm so privileged to travel around and still get up in the morning and say, 'Yes! I'm going to umpire again today.' Back in the old days, when I was working for the Railways, I would get up and think, 'Oh shit, I have to go and sit in the office today.' All my life I have been one for the sun and open air, so what better job than umpiring?

I have always said I'll carry on as long as I enjoy the game. On the morning of a match day I still get excited about the prospect of umpiring and I can't wait to start. On my free days I hang around the hotel or go and play golf, when I get the chance. But after all these years I would still rather be out in the middle every day of the week.

There's a lot of pressure on an umpire out there, which you can either crack under or thrive on. You can't allow the strain to get to you, or you'll be in trouble. I have always tried to remain as calm as possible and not to get ruffled by anything that happens on the field. Of course, at times it's easier said than done, but you have to stay cool, and the more experience you gain over the years, the better you can handle the pressure. If you are able to concentrate very hard for very long, you will hopefully make fewer mistakes.

Believe me, in the modern age, where television technology checks your every move through replays from various angles, umpiring is not an easy job. But you have to accept that it's only human to make mistakes now and then. Mistakes *will* happen, no matter how good an umpire you are. The important thing is to try to learn from them and not to repeat them.

Even in my 100th Test, at Lord's in the 2009 Ashes, my life was not made any easier by the players and the fans. Cricket is an immensely intense game at times, and none more so than in Ashes cricket. I realised beforehand that it would be a tough match, and that's how it was. But I believe that pressure actually makes you better; it forces you to concentrate harder, and I managed to survive the match.

In the past the Australians, in particular, have been accused of pressuring umpires excessively, especially when they're appealing. But it's not just the Australians; the Sri Lankans, Indians … you name them … they all appeal vociferously at times. In fact, the same applies to cricket at all levels, whether club, provincial or Test cricket. If players think that they can break you down, they will surely try. When you hear some of the appeals, you can't help thinking, 'It *must* be out.' And once you've made the decision and it's wrong, they know they've got you. From there on in they'll try to break you down in the run of the day, as well as the next day and the day after that. But an umpire actually needs the pressure. What's the point of standing there for five days, relaxing, and nothing ever happens? You won't enjoy it as much, will you?

In the 2005 Ashes, when the weather was dicey and Kevin Pietersen scored that 158, Shane Warne came on and started pressuring me, saying things like, 'I *have* to bowl England out,' as if expecting me to help make that happen!

The players do get frustrated sometimes and they find it difficult to hide their emotions. In a match between Australia and the West Indies some time ago, Daryl Harper turned down a few appeals from Australian leg spinner Stuart MacGill for lbws against the Windies batsmen, who didn't bother to offer any shots. Frustrated, MacGill told Daryl that 'you should use your brain more often'!

I always strive for a good rapport with the players. I'm one of the umpires who allows them a little bit of banter on the field. Sledging used to be bad, but since the ICC introduced heavy fines for swearing and verbal intimidation to improve the game's image, the situation has improved. By all accounts, the Aussies were the worst in the past. One of the best I've heard from another umpire was when a young Proteas batsman stepped to the crease and the Aussie captain told his bowler, 'Don't be too hard on him, he's still breastfeeding.' Another occurred when an opposing batsman was cheaply dismissed and he was sent off with the words 'Back to the nets, you idiot!' In my 100th Test, at Lord's, the spirit between the sides was amazingly docile, considering what was at stake.

To me it's important to have the respect of the players, and I try to show them respect too. Sometimes I go and watch the guys practising in the nets a few days before a match, and it's a good feeling when I hear a player say, 'Look, here's Rudi, he's umpiring the Test. Good to see you.'

When I'm on the field among the players, I prefer to be by myself most of the time so that I can concentrate on the play. But now and then, when they want to chat, I speak to the guys and have a bit of fun with them. You can't just stand there in your own little cocoon all day – sometimes you have to relax a little. In the last Lord's Test, for instance, I was watching Freddie Flintoff and could see he was struggling. As he walked past me, he said, 'Rudi, I'm getting old now. I'm battling.' I told him, 'Just hang in there; keep going. You're still all right, you know.' And he finished with a fine performance.

But I will only talk to the players when they approach me. Some will come and have a chat, asking me how I am, where I have just come from and where I am off to after the match.

I have never been one to shy away from apologising when I know I have made an umpiring error, at any level of cricket. I have heard umpires say that they never apologise, as there was nothing deliberate about the errors they'd made, and that the replays will show their mistakes, anyway (unlike the old days, when umpires got away with anything). I can remember as far back as 1992, in a Nissan Shield match between Free State and

Border, when I gave out the promising Free State batsman Louis Wilkinson as run out when he was on 91. I thought he'd had his bat in the air, but I was wrong. I realised that I had effectively robbed him of his first century of the season, so I apologised to him afterwards. It doesn't cost you anything to say you're sorry, and the players appreciate and respect you more for it.

When Australia played England in the first Test at Lord's in 2005, I apologised to Brett Lee after he had hit Kevin Pietersen with a thigh-high full toss on day three and I didn't give him out. Lee was bowling magnificently at the time. Looking for the yorker, he sent off a scorching delivery at Pietersen's foot, but it went higher than expected and instead hit his leg in front of the stumps. I just lost sight of the ball at the last moment, and it cost Lee a wicket. I apologised to him afterwards, and he took it in good spirit.

In 2007, in a match between Australia and Sri Lanka, I gave out Kumar Sangakkara caught by Ricky Ponting in the slips when he was on 192 and approaching his seventh Test double hundred. Replays showed that the ball had, in fact, come off his shoulder. I knew how disappointed he must have felt and I went up to him afterwards and apologised for my decision. Kumar didn't make a fuss about it. As his captain, Mahela Jayawardene, once said, when you look back after your dismissal, 'you know it's a mistake made by a human and that's it'.

Umpires are always in the firing line for the decisions they make, and the players, the press, the fans and the rest of humankind will all criticise you. It is, unfortunately, one of the lows of cricket umpiring that we just have to live with. No one enjoys being criticised, and cricket umpires are no exception. But criticism is around all the time; we get criticised about as much as the players do. One has to grow quite thick-skinned to survive, but there comes a time in many people's lives when things become *too* much.

In 2001, BC Cooray of Sri Lanka and I were heavily criticised in BC's last outing before he retired from umpiring. We had been standing in the second Test match between England and Sri Lanka in Kandy, when all hell broke loose after the match due to certain decisions we'd taken. Ironically, the dust had just been settling on the controversial first Test in Galle, after which the newspapers had reported that they hoped BC and I, the umpires in the second Test, would 'be stronger in mind' than our Galle counterparts. England's Alec Stewart, for instance, called the lbw decision that went against him in the first innings of the first Test in Galle 'the worst I have ever received in any form of cricket', which was quite a statement to make.

In the second Test, BC and I had a bad day at the office. During the match, tempers flared when some of the players accused one another of dishonesty, and at one stage Kumar Sangakkara and Michael Atherton were involved in a vicious verbal confrontation. I didn't have the best of umpiring days myself, but BC said afterwards, 'It has easily been the worst game I have ever had in my 23-year career. No umpire goes into a match [wanting] to make mistakes, but a lot of them happened.' Afterwards poor BC was cruelly nicknamed 'Bad Call Cooray'.

Believe me when I say that umpiring a cricket game on the Indian subcontinent is not easy. The climate is very demanding and the light very bright, which puts quite a strain on the eyes. Pitches are prepared for spinners, as the ball spins a lot on these pitches, and spinners are plentiful. Because of this, there are a lot more bat–pad incidents.

Players from the subcontinent also appeal a *lot* and for almost anything, which puts a lot of pressure on the umpires. We have to put the players in their place from the start. Four years ago, for example, when India played Pakistan in the first Test in Mohali, Darrell Hair and I reported India paceman Lakshmipathy Balaji for excessive appealing, even though he achieved career-best figures of 9/171. We felt he had overstepped the mark, and match referee Chris Broad agreed. Balaji was fined 30 per cent of his match fee.

Because of the extensive travelling we umpires do, fatigue is often blamed when we make errors. Although this may certainly be true for some and not others, it's not inconceivable that criss-crossing the globe – not to mention the sheer number of matches – takes its toll. Not so long ago, the Emirates Elite Panel was struggling along with just seven members.

Over the years an umpire's workload has increased significantly. Let me give you an example of how things have changed. Between 1981 and 1990, the well-known Dickie Bird umpired for a total of 167 days, averaging 16 days a year. From 1981 to 1985, the Australian Mel Johnson, then the busiest international umpire, stood 23 days a year on average. From 1991 to 1995, an umpire's workload remained fairly light, but then the ICC came up with their 10-year schedule, umpires could no longer officiate in Tests in which their own country played and a neutral umpire also had to be on-field in every ODI. Suddenly, the itinerary for inter-national umpires was very full. In the four years between 1996 and 1999, for example, Steve Bucknor stood 43 days a year on average, while in 2004 I stood 71 days and Steve Bucknor 70 days; in 2005 alone, Billy Bowden stood 73 days, Aleem Dar and Steve Bucknor 63 days, and I 61 days.

Estimates indicate that the world's top cricketers play around 70 to 90 days in a year, but they have the luxury of putting up their feet on the players' balcony for a fair part of the game, which we as umpires don't. And then people think only the players suffer from a packed itinerary! It's a good thing that the membership on the Elite Panel has been somewhat increased. It will allow umpires to officiate in fewer games, travel less and spend more quality time with their families at home. My family has become used to my absence, as I've been doing the job for so many years. Sometimes I think I'm just a nuisance when I get home! In jest they will ask, 'When do you leave again?'

I look at the young guys coming through the system now, some younger than 40, and it's good to see. They have many years still to umpire, but I feel sorry for them about only one thing, and that is that they all have young kids. I've been umpiring at international level for 17 years. My oldest son, Rudolf, is 28, and his brother, Luan, is 25, and I've never had much special time with them. Sometimes you think about all the good times you could have had with the family, but fortunately mine know just how much I love the game and they have never begrudged me my career and have lived with its concomitant sacrifices.

It is as hard for umpires to travel extensively and spend idle time doing nothing – waiting for flights at airports, for example – as it is for professional cricketers. But at least players are in a team environment, whereas umpires are largely left to their own devices.

Because of all the travelling and having to stand on your feet for hours at a time for days in a row, you have to ensure that you stay fit or you won't survive. I go to the gym for an hour and a half on the days I'm off and also run or cycle almost every day. I find that being fit really helps to get me through a six-hour day. Of course, exercising is not always possible when you are travelling, but I always try to fit something in. I also play golf whenever I get the chance. Many years ago I used to go fishing, but on one occasion the Beach Buggy got stuck and we had to walk back for miles in the loose sand, which killed that sport for me!

I also make sure that I'm well prepared for matches. I go and stand in the nets a day or two before the start of a game to get focused on the ball and observe the bowlers. Now and then a new lad comes on the scene you've never seen bowl before, so you don't know what he does with the ball. I observe what kind of balls he bowls or, if he's a batsman, what sort of shots he plays. Then, when I go out onto the field in the match, I at least know what to expect.

On a couple of occasions I've also discovered that umpiring is not always a safe job. I've mentioned the Pakistan/New Zealand series in Pakistan in 2002. Pakistan was on a high, having won the first Test in Lahore by an innings and 324 runs. But we never got to the second Test. On 8 May a bomb went off close to the hotel in Karachi where the officials and teams were staying, killing 14 people. At the time of the explosion I was elsewhere in town, buying a few nice rugs for our home.

When I got back to my hotel room, I was shocked by the scene of destruction that greeted me. One had to see it to believe it. I couldn't comprehend the force of an explosion that had blown the door and large window of my room completely out of their frames; shattered glass lay everywhere. I had to shake bits and pieces of broken glass from the clothes I had left lying on the bed before I went out. I shuddered as I imagined what could have happened had I been inside the room at the time of the blast.

We, the match officials, were told to pack as quickly as possible, and that same evening match referee Mike Procter and I flew back to South Africa. The other umpire, Steve Bucknor, and Stephen Fleming's men also got on the plane the same day. Understandably, the rest of New Zealand's tour was cancelled. We knew that the Pakistan Cricket Board had worked very hard to ensure that sufficient safety measures were in place during the tour, but, nevertheless, this horrible thing still happened.

Unfortunately, the way in which the Kiwis and some of the ICC officials were treated after the event caused a lot of anger, as we were basically left to fend for ourselves. Several members of the PCB had panicked after the bomb blast and simply disappeared. The person in charge of the team officials left for Lahore on an early-evening flight along with his colleagues, leaving me, Mike Procter and Steve Bucknor behind. We did not know what the hell was going on. Fortunately the liaison officer of the New Zealand team later rescued us, and he arranged for us to fly to Dubai on an Emirates flight at 11 that night.

I had another uncomfortable experience in April 2006, in Guwahati, the main city of India's north-eastern state of Assam.

From what I'd heard the place had been racked by ethnic violence for over two decades. I was there just before the final phase of elections to the state assembly, and with the authorities expecting possible violence, heavy security was provided for the players and officials.

I was due to stand in the fifth ODI between India and England, with India leading the seven-match series 4-0. Heavy overnight rain had left the outfield soaking wet, and at some stage a helicopter was pressed into action to try to dry out the ground, all to no avail. My co-umpire Arani Jayaprakash and I made four inspections before we decided that it was hopeless – no play at all would be possible.

But cricket supporters had been sitting at the stadium all day waiting for the game to start. Some of them had arrived at the ground as early as 5 a.m. after having travelled long distances to see the game. They hadn't had any cricket for years, and they were getting more and more frustrated and, eventually, agitated, until their frustration erupted into violence. They started throwing all kinds of missiles, set advertising hoardings on fire, tore down some of the fencing to enter the ground and even pelted the TV cameras with stones. The police, who had to step in to try to restore some order, were attacked with water bottles, stones and bamboo poles, and they fired several rounds of tear gas to chase the crowd away from the stadium. In the chaos, both spectators and policemen were injured. One of the policemen lay unconscious after being hit by a stone. Of course the cricket officials and players had security personnel protection, but even so it was a tense time for everyone.

When fans get overexcited, you never know how badly things can get out of hand. I remember a Nissan Shield match at Newlands some 20 years ago, when Western Province played Transvaal, and I was standing with Karl Liebenberg. Western Province only needed one more wicket to win the match, with Richard Snell and Rod Estwick at the crease. Snell skyed a ball to fine leg, and while

Terence Lazard was waiting to take the catch, the spectators ran onto the field, anticipating a clean catch.

With spectators all over the place, the two batsmen ran a few runs. Officials requested the crowd to stay off the field, but when Estwick hit a ball in the same direction soon after, the same thing happened. Karl and I had to stop play until we were satisfied that matters were more or less under control. Transvaal skipper Clive Rice was furious, saying that his players would simply walk off the field in future should the same thing happen again at Newlands.

I also remember that dreadful day in early March 2009, when I heard the shocking news that the Sri Lankan cricket team had been attacked by 12 masked men armed with rifles, rocket launchers and grenades close to the Gaddafi Stadium in Lahore. In the attack on their team bus, six players were injured, along with their British assistant coach Paul Farbrace. Kumar Sangakkara, whom I gave out by mistake in 2007, was one of the injured players. But, worse than that, six police officers and two civilians were killed.

Ironically, the Sri Lankan team were in Pakistan only because India had pulled out of a Test series following the Mumbai terror attacks.

A minivan following the team bus, carrying the match referee and umpires, was also fired upon and the driver was killed. Umpires Simon Taufel, Steve Davis, Nadeem Ghauri and Ahsan Raza, umpires' performance manager Peter Manuel, liaison officer Abdul Sami and ICC match referee Chris Broad were in this minivan. Umpire Ahsan Raza was hit by a bullet and bled profusely from a chest wound, and Chris Broad tried to stop the bleeding by covering the wound with his hand. A policeman who climbed into the van to seek cover at first refused to drive it, but after Broad insisted vociferously, he drove them to safety.

It was clear that the situation in Pakistan would not allow teams to travel to the country in the immediate future. The ICC had been assured on many occasions that cricketers would never be targeted in Pakistan, but this event now proved that not to be the case. It was even more disturbing to learn that an alternative route was taken to the stadium because the police had been warned about a possible attack on the team. Yet the attack still happened. One of the main questions that arose from the incident was, of course, whether Pakistan would still co-host the 2011 World Cup along with India, Bangladesh and Sri Lanka. Eventually it was decided that only India, Sri Lanka and Bangladesh would host the event, with Mumbai as the venue for the final.

Sometimes a situation can be both funny and not so funny at the same time. I recall a match at St George's Park in Port Elizabeth that had to be suspended for a day – in the middle of summer in 1995, in almost perfect cricket weather – because of the revelry of some inebriated wedding guests. Western Province was playing Eastern Province in a Castle Currie Cup match, and at the time they needed a win to remain in the hunt for the final.

When I arrived at the ground on the Sunday morning – the second day of the match, if I recall correctly – I was greeted by the sight of groundsmen trying their best to dry out almost half of the pitch at the Duckpond End, which was totally drenched. It emerged that the president's lounge had been rented out for a wedding on the Saturday night, and the guests had one hell of a party. When an Eastern Province Cricket Union official went to investigate noise coming from the field, he discovered some of the guests, most of them almost naked, wearing only tangas, skidding merrily up and down the wet pitch covers. It took a while for the official to persuade the merrymakers to get off the covers and away from the pitch.

But, oh dear, it was then discovered that the covers had shifted during all the sliding and water had seeped onto the pitch. So, in the early hours of the morning until lunch time, everything was done to try to soak up the water and dry out the soil, including a trick borrowed from the West Indies – setting fuel alight on the damp parts. But, alas, we had no choice but to postpone the match until the next morning.

Of course the Western Province chaps weren't impressed, but the Eastern Province Cricket Union refused to take any responsibility for the mishap. And there were probably some people in the Friendly City who thought the match postponement even funnier than their antics of the night before!

The game of cricket has changed a lot over the years and, in the modern era, we find that music and dancing and all kinds of entertainment have become part of the sport. Some of these events have become real festivals and seem to be overshadowed only by the yearly carnival in Rio. Twenty years ago, already, there was some dancing too – by umpires. Who can forget Barry Lambson, the slim, loose-jointed umpire from Transvaal, who made the 'Lambson Lambada' famous?

As I recall, the dance originated during the Nissan Shield limited-overs competition. According to a new format of the competition, teams could make use of substitutes, and the umpire had to indicate a substitution from the middle of the pitch to the scorekeepers, while the tune of the sponsors blared over the loudspeakers. And so, every time Barry signalled a substitution, he would sway his hips to the rhythm of the tune, to the great delight of the spectators. Thus the Lambson Lambada was born. Some fans even dubbed Barry 'Travolta' Lambson! I was standing with Barry in a match in Bloemfontein once when Northern Transvaal all-rounder Anton Ferreira added some spice to the ritual and joined in, using his bat as a fiddle. The crowd loved it even more.

I tried the lambada once in a game at the Wanderers between Transvaal and Natal, but the cricket bosses told me not to do it again. Apparently some of the more conservative guys at the top didn't like it. There were fears that Barry's dancing career would be nipped in the bud as well, but fortunately that didn't happen. These days New Zealand umpire Billy Bowden's actions do a lot to entertain the spectators, especially his signalling of a six, a big favourite with crowds around the world.

Once in a while one reads about professional sportspeople who suffer food poisoning or pick up debilitating viruses while on tour. One such case supposedly occurred during the 1995 Rugby World Cup in South Africa, when it was alleged that the All Blacks had been deliberately poisoned before the final in Johannesburg (the perpetrator was named as 'Susie'). In the cricket world, players touring overseas are often the victims of food poisoning. I once suffered a similar fate in Johannesburg in the worst case of my life, and witnessed the biggest devastation in a team context in all my years of umpiring. I may add that it was before the days of 'Susie', somewhere around 1993.

England A was touring South Africa at the time, and they were on a roll after three successive wins. Then they played Jimmy Cook's Transvaal side in a four-day match at the Wanderers, where I stood with Cyril Mitchley. Cyril lived in Johannesburg, while I was staying at the Sandton Hotel, along with the England players.

I was the first victim, hit on the second day of the match already. Hardly half an hour into the match I started feeling dizzy. I couldn't even see the flight of the ball properly, which of course is the last thing any umpire can afford. I spoke to Cyril and the captain about my dilemma and there was only one thing to do – go off. At the tea break, England A captain Hugh Morris and his opening batting partner, Mark Lathwell, also complained of not feeling too well.

My condition didn't improve over the course of the day, but that night I slept it off and was back behind the stumps the next day – but only at one o'clock, as seven of the England match XI were out of action with the same virus! Jimmy Cook had wanted to give them time to recover, and eventually some of the ill players did manage to drag themselves onto the field. However, team manager Phil Neale, physio Wayne Morton and three of the players not chosen for the original XI had to stand in for the sick cricketers. Tour manager Bob Bennett later told me that they had

had an even worse experience in Kenya five years earlier, when only four England players had been left standing. The scheduled one-day match had to be called off. Cyril Mitchley and I both agreed that in our long careers as umpires we had never experienced an interruption of play such as this!

The great thing about cricket is that you meet a lot of characters. Among the players and umpires that immediately come to mind are Pat Symcox, Brian McMillan, Lou Rautenbach – whom I mentioned in the Alvin Kallicharran episode in another chapter – Dave Shepherd and Billy Bowden, to name but a few.

I remember the day when Lou, standing in a two-day club match at the University of Port Elizabeth (UPE), arrived at the ground without the match ball on the final day, a Sunday. Calling time on the Saturday evening, he had apparently taken the match ball and put it in his coat pocket. But when he arrived at the ground the next morning, he could not find the ball anywhere. It was an hour before play would start, so Lou – who lives on a farm about 130 kilometres from Port Elizabeth – phoned his wife Marie, who said she had found the ball at home. They agreed to meet each other halfway, at the town of Addo, where Marie would hand over the ball. Lou drove out to Addo and back at a hell of a lick and managed to get back to the UPE ground with 10 minutes to spare – only to find that the innings had been declared!

Former umpire Dave Shepherd, who sadly died in 2009, was one of the most popular chaps on the international circuit until his retirement in 2005. He once missed three wicket-taking no-balls as Pakistan came back to beat England at Old Trafford in 2001, and his colleagues jokingly used to remind him of his oversight afterwards. At first his mistakes did bother him and he came close to quitting, but he was persuaded to stay on. Dave was famous for being superstitious. Whenever the number 111 or its multiples appeared on the scoreboard, he would hop around on one leg every few seconds until the score changed. I umpired my first Test in 1992 with the good-humoured Dave, and I always had the greatest admiration for him.

I hope that one day they can say the same about me as some-one at Worcester county wrote about Dave: 'For him cricket was a lovely game, a simple game and a game to be enjoyed. He himself brought so much enjoyment to so many of us.'

14

The future of the game

"*A T20 game comes and goes very quickly, and whereas there is the satisfaction and thrill of performing in front of big crowds, to a genuine world-class player his record in first-class cricket is still the one that matters the most. It is the final benchmark by which he will be judged.*"

What does the future hold for cricket and all its different formats? I think the sport has never been healthier than it is now, which I ascribe to the fact that it is in very capable hands. It offers three excellent formats that make it possible for everyone to find an option to go and enjoy. After extensive trial and error, the game is also embracing technology at the right time. The umpire decision review system, or decision review system, effective since 1 October 2009, will help umpires to make more correct decisions, which should please players and fans alike.

The new craze in cricket, of course, is Twenty20, and there's no doubt that this format is here to stay. Because we live in a fast-paced, pressurised world, many people don't have the time to watch an entire five-day cricket match, and then only to see it grind into a draw at the end. For many spectators, Test cricket lacks fun and excitement, whereas Twenty20 has it all. The Twenty20

Cup was the original form of the 20-over game, and people were both amused and sceptical when it was launched in 2003. But attendance figures of the format have since dramatically increased.

There are many who believe that, with the growing popularity of Twenty20, Test cricket, and even one-day cricket, will suffer, as fewer and fewer people will show up to watch Test matches – which, economically, would not be in the game's interests. Yet I believe that traditional, classic cricket will prevail. Recent attendance figures at Test matches in Australia, England and South Africa alone reveal that Test cricket is still very much alive.

It is a fact that the real skills and endurance of cricketers are not tested in Twenty20 matches to anywhere near the same degree as they are in Test matches, as a Twenty20 game finishes within three hours, while Test cricket involves whole days of play. Twenty-over cricket by itself will not provide the player with the time to develop and nurture the skills he is going to require at the highest level. These skills must still be acquired on the provincial or county circuit. I have heard several Australian and South African players say that the English county circuit is the best cricket finishing school in the world.

I believe a player takes much more satisfaction in scoring a century in a four- or five-day match than blasting a rapid 50 in a 20-over affair. Both the player and the selectors will always study his four- or five-day record before they look at anything else: how many runs he has accumulated, and at what average.

In T20, luck, and not necessarily skills, plays a major role, which is why it is so difficult to predict a winner in the IPL, for instance. In 2008, Shane Warne's Rajasthan Royals were the cheapest franchise at US$67 million (the Jaipur franchise was even penalised for underbidding during the auctions). A team lacking in real star value, they were thought to be dead in the water. But all that flew out the window once the tournament got underway, and in the end the Rajasthan Royals won the trophy.

By contrast, at the player auctions the Royal Challengers

Bangalore picked cricketers better known for their Test skills, and the strategy misfired from match one, the side eventually finishing seventh. A guy like Jacques Kallis, for example, was bought for a whopping $900 000, but he just couldn't get going.

Batsmen swing at every ball in T20, and therefore even an average batsman can hit a quick 50. And a mediocre bowler by Test standards can suddenly take four or five wickets. In Test cricket, though, the same player may not perform this well consistently, as the format requires exceptional skills and a strong mental attitude.

I have watched players at the crease at international level for 17 years and I know from experience that batsmen take great pleasure in batting for long periods of time, while bowlers relish long bowling spells. They have time to play or bowl themselves in, the batsmen don't have to rush their strokes and the bowlers can work on a bowling strategy to get a particular batsman out.

In T20, however, a batsman may reckon he has had a good innings if he batted for some 30-odd balls, and a bowler can only send down a maximum of 24 deliveries. A T20 game comes and goes very quickly, and whereas there is the satisfaction and thrill of performing in front of big crowds, to a genuine world-class player his record in first-class cricket is still the one that matters the most. It is the final benchmark by which he will be judged.

Ian Chappell, former Australian captain and now cricket commentator, recently suggested that a three-day Test match be introduced in order to 'save' Test cricket, which drew an interesting response from the fans. He – and I – found it enlightening to hear that cricket fans did not like his idea at all – they did not want anyone to tamper with Test cricket. From the fans' response, we can gauge that there is still a lot of passion for the longer version of the game.

Chappell's proposal to revamp Test cricket – 'cricket's global-warming challenge', as he calls it – entails a World Test championship among the eight major nations to decide the No. 1-ranked side in the world (at the time of writing, this was Australia).

According to Chappell, the secret to a series of three-day Tests is finding a ball that will facilitate day–night Tests – cricket engineers are working on this – and to then play three seven-hour days of cricket. He believes that if the administrators and players can agree to compromise on a few issues, then 16 overs an hour are feasible. From our experience as umpires this won't be easy, and I was immediately interested to see what 'compromises' he had in mind.

He did list them: clear, full-sized sight boards, no TV replays to decide boundaries, a back-foot no-ball law to eradicate over-stepping, ball boys beyond the ropes, and strictly controlling the duration of unofficial drinks breaks on the field. Should a team fall behind the 16-overs-an-hour rate, the captain will be suspended from playing in the next championship game.

One of my immediate concerns was the new DRS, which slows the game down, but Chappell suggested it be activated only when the third umpire overrules 'an absolute howler'.

If all of the above 'compromises' can be realised, Chappell says, the championship games would amount to bowling about the same number of balls as is bowled in a modern Test of four days.

Rather than a computer determining a team's world ranking, as is done now, the championship would be a far more interesting way in which to crown the number-one Test team in the world. The matches could be played over a weekend – Friday, Saturday and Sunday – when fans are more likely to attend, also allowing players plenty of time to rest between matches. And the format will appeal to TV, as weekends are the most popular sporting days and play is virtually guaranteed on all days.

We all know how drawn out any cricket championship, including the World Cup, can be, so being able to crown a victor in the minimum amount of time is also significant.

Other crucial aspects of Chappell's plan include prize money and a points system that must generously reward outright victory, pitches that must ensure a balance between bat and ball, and games played at venues where the chances of rain are slim (remember the 2007 World Cup?). Chappell also proposes eradicating not-outs so that batsmen don't focus too intently on their averages, and that perhaps the championship statistics should not be included with those of traditional Test matches.

Limiting the match to three days and providing more rest days in between will result in additional spin-offs: it might encourage more genuine fast bowling; a good part of the match would be played in the cool of the evening, when the bowlers and fielders feel fresher; it will challenge captains tactically to find quicker ways to gain results; and it will make for a more aggressive approach, which would attract more fans to the ground. What Test cricket needs to survive, says Chappell, is a balance between 'what satisfies the players and what excites the fans'.

He surely has a point, but whether the cricketing authorities will agree with him remains to be seen.

Lately there have been suggestions that, if anything, 50-over cricket is more under threat than Test cricket. Domestic cricket in South Africa has introduced a 40-overs game, but it has yet to prove itself a better option than the 50-over format. At the end of the 2009 ICC Champions Trophy, hosted in South Africa, Australian captain Ricky Ponting, whose team won the tournament, and Brendon McCullum, stand-in captain for the other finalist, New Zealand, both said that the championship had done much to ensure that the 50-over game will remain alive and well.

'There's plenty of space for both 20-over cricket and 50-over cricket to fit in alongside the Test game,' Ponting said. 'The Test game is the form of the game I enjoy the most, but 50-over cricket, with tournaments like this [the ICC Championship], will certainly hold its own. I was worried at the time when 20-over cricket became as popular as it did that we might start playing fewer 50-over games, but I think tournaments like this can only help the game.'

Ponting also made an important point regarding the duration of the tournament and the number of teams involved. For the first time, the championship had been reduced to eight teams. 'We've only been here a couple of weeks and the tournament's over,' he said. 'You've got the best eight teams in the world playing for it ...'

McCullum said, 'I thought this tournament was good. The top eight teams in the world coming together and playing over a short period of time; I thought it worked well ... If 50-over cricket is to remain on the calendar, it's a great way to certainly push it with tournaments like the Champions Trophy.'

The last World Cup in 2007 suffered exactly the opposite of what these two players rated as positives of the Champions Trophy: 16 teams competing, of which some, with all respect, didn't belong on the same parks as the likes of, say, Australia and Sri Lanka; and a long-winded tournament as a result. By the time the semis and the final arrived, it had just gone on for too long. For me, this is where the danger lies in the future of the World Cup.

If you compare the Twenty20 competition with the World Cup, in many ways the former has a lot more to offer than the latter. T20 is fast-paced, explosive and guarantees a result every time, while the spectators are treated to constant fun. T20 cricket is, more than anything, a festival. From my experience, people don't care much for wickets; they first of all come to watch fours and sixes being hit. And they get it, plenty.

In addition, the huge amounts of money to be earned in the IPL and similar tournaments almost guarantee that the top players will make an appearance. Before the 2009 Stanford tournament, rumours abounded that some of England's leading cricketers, such as Kevin Pietersen and Andrew Flintoff, had threatened not to sign their central contracts, preferring to play in India. It even seemed possible that some players would retire from their national duties and throw in their lot with the IPL, such was the lure of big money. (In September 2009, Flintoff would become the world's first full-time freelance cricketer.)

I first stood in the IPL tournament of 2008. The event had everything for the spectators, and after the spectacular opening ceremony, the first match, in which I umpired on-field, got off with a bang as Kolkata's Brendon McCullum smashed a record unbeaten 158 off 73 balls, with 13 sixes and 10 fours. It also brought a relatively unknown cricketer to the fore, which is another plus for the format. Australian Shaun Marsh scored over 600 runs in 11 matches, including a whirlwind 115 against the Rajasthan Royals. Everyone was asking why he hasn't played for Australia yet. And the joke was that he was bought for a mere $30 000, so he was by far the best bargain of the tournament. An incentive for new players would now be to perform well in their domestic seasons so that they can eventually get into the IPL.

With the IPL having taken off like a rocket, the same could not be said for its rival, the breakaway Indian Cricket League (ICL). The ICL came about in 2007, bankrolled by India's largest media Group, Zee Television, and ran parallel to the Indian Premier League (IPL), which is managed by the Board of Control for Cricket in India (BCCI). The ICL followed the Twenty20 format, while there was also a domestic 50-over tournament.

Matches were initially held at Panchula near Chandigarh, in Hyderabad and in Gugaon near New Delhi, but in 2008 games were played at more venues across India. Players participating in this league were threatened with bans by the cricket boards of their respective countries, as the ICL was regarded as an un-sanctioned rebel league, unrecognised by the board of the BCCI and the ICC.

By the end of 2009, outstanding monies to players and umpires amounted to millions of dollars. It seemed fairly certain that even if payments were made, anyone previously contracted to the ICL would think twice before recommitting themselves to the league. Most were tired of the empty promises and the various excuses they'd heard every month for a year.

When it became apparent to the players that there was no

money with which to pay them, they handed the matter over to the Federation of International Cricketers' Associations (FICA). FICA and the players were apparently regularly informed that payments would be made and provided with dates on which this would happen, but nothing ever came of it. The only way forward seemed to be legal action. The CEO of FICA, Tim May, made it clear that even if the ICL received official recognition, it would struggle to lure players in future. With the league's history and the way in which it treated players, 'no player will want to play in it,' he said in a statement. 'They will have to win back the trust of the playing community, and that is why they must pay the outstanding wages.'

One of the players to whom the league owed big money was former Proteas all-rounder Andrew Hall, who had played for the Chandigarh Lions. Hall declared that even if the ICL paid him the outstanding amount for his current contract as well as the full amount upfront for a new one, he would never again play for the league. He was particularly aggrieved because he had given up his international career to play for the ICL – he could have been useful to the Proteas in 2009/10 – and had refused an IPL contract offered to him at the same time in favour of the ICL.

South African ICL players Hall (Dolphins), Johan van der Wath (Diamond Eagles) and Justin Kemp (Cape Cobras) have resumed their careers in South Africa, while Lance Klusener (formerly Dolphins) is now a bowling coach at his former franchise.

Some may say that the guys were just plain greedy, but that's not for us to judge. There may be a lesson to be learnt from this saga, though, especially for the younger players, who just look at the dollars offered to them and little else.

While the IPL and such tournaments have their place, I think there should be a proper balance between traditional Test cricket, the 50-over game and Twenty20 cricket. As the Tri-Nations and Super 14 tournaments have shown in rugby, the more you have of something, the less valuable it becomes. Because of the frequency with which they take place, even contests between the Springboks and the All Blacks, once legendary, have become less exciting.

For the sake of all formats of cricket, the game should not be overplayed and its value reduced in the process. The ICC will have to give this issue serious consideration, and it will be one of the biggest challenges they face in the future: to find the perfect balance.

15

Records and runs

" *Personally I feel the old body still has a few years of umpiring left in it, and I would like to go on until at least the 2011 World Cup. As mentioned before, I still haven't stood on-field in a World Cup final, which I would dearly love to do. Whatever happens, at the end of the day I will be able to look back on a wonderful time spent in a wonderful sport.* "

My last Tests for the season involved the Pakistan tour of New Zealand and Australia, contested from November 2009 to January 2010. I was TV umpire for the first Test at the University Oval in Dunedin, where the Kiwis took a 1-0 lead in the three-Test series after scoring 429 in their first innings – and that after opener McIntosh was bowled first ball. One's heart bled for Kiwi skipper Daniel Vettori, who lost his wicket on 99 when he tried to run Akmal down to third man but got a thick edge through to the keeper. For a top-order batsman it may be just one of those things if he doesn't make a century, but if you bat at No. 8, you don't often get the opportunity to reach a hundred.

Pakistan levelled the series in the second Test in Wellington (where I stood on-field with Simon Taufel), winning convincingly by 141 runs after Mohammad Asif took an outstanding 5/67.

The third Test in Napier, where I was again in charge on-field along with Billy Doctrove, was drawn, but it did produce some interesting cricket. Pakistan was bowled out for 223 in their first innings, with opening batsman Imran Farhat on 117 after Yousuf, Akmal, Misbah-ul-Haq and Asif had all gone for ducks. This time Vettori did get his hundred (134 off 186 balls). New Zealand's total was 471, despite Danish Kaneria once again producing a great spell, with 7/168. Tail-ender Chris Martin also scored his 28th Test duck! Pakistan then replied with 455, setting New Zealand a modest target of 208 runs, but on 90 without loss, still needing only 118 from a minimum of 23 overs, rain unfortunately had the final say to end the Kiwis' hopes of a series win.

From New Zealand I crossed the Tasman Sea to Australia, where the Aussies were eagerly waiting for Pakistan after their 2-0 home-series win against the West Indies. I stood in the first Test in Melbourne with Billy Doctrove, and in several ways it became a landmark Test. Australia scored 454 in their first innings, with Simon Katich caught on 98 and Shane Watson run out on 93. Pakistan replied with a mediocre 258, but they bowled out the Aussies for 225 in their second innings. Seventeen-year-old Pakistan bowler Mohammad Aamer took 5/79 to become the youngest fast bowler in Test cricket history to claim five wickets (only left-arm spinner Nasim-ul-Ghani achieved the feat at a younger age, against the West Indians more than 50 years ago).

At the close of the Australian innings, opener Shane Watson was still not out on 120 – but what agony to get there! He first saw off the last over before lunch from Saeed Ajmal to break on an unbeaten 98, but there were some anxious moments after lunch when he chased a succession of wide deliveries outside his off-stump. On 99, he slashed a full, wide delivery from Aamer to Rauf in the gully, who dropped it, allowing Watson to scamper through for his maiden Test hundred. It took him just over an hour from the time he'd reached 90 to get to his century – so here was a very relieved man!

At 170/3, Pakistan looked on course for victory, but a great over by Johnson, in which he claimed two wickets in succession, knocked them back. With Nathan Hauritz pitching in with 5/101, Pakistan finally slumped to 251 all out – 170 runs short of their target.

For Australian captain Ricky Ponting it was a most memorable Test. He broke the record for the most wins by any Test player and the most wins for any Test captain. The win over Pakistan took Ponting to 93 Test victories, passing Shane Warne's record of 92. It also gave him his 42nd win as Test captain, surpassing Steve Waugh's previous record.

The second Test at the Sydney Cricket Ground, where I acted as TV umpire, was one of the most remarkable I have ever seen. Scoring a poor 127 in their first innings, when Mohammad Asif wrecked their batting effort, the Australians were staring down the barrel. Pakistan's first-innings score of 333 meant that Australia was trailing by more than 200 runs. By the end of Day 3, they were only 80 runs ahead, with two wickets in hand. Danish Kaneria, who five years before took a seven-wicket haul against Australia at the same ground, had already taken four wickets by then. Fortunately for the Aussies, Mike Hussey was still at the crease on 73, thanks to the generosity of Pakistan wicketkeeper Kamran Akmal, who'd dropped him three times off the bowling of Kaneria. After 33 gruelling overs, Kaneria had to be carried off the field late in the day with suspected leg cramps.

The next day Hussey went on to score 138 not out, and with the help of tail-ender Peter Siddle, who contributed 38, took Australia's total to 381 all out. That left Pakistan to score a mere 176 runs, with more than a day to achieve it. It should have been a formality, and at 50/1 they looked well on course. But Nathan Hauritz (5/53) and Mitchell Johnson (3/27) blew them away, and after only 38 overs Pakistan were back in the pavilion for 139. With that, Ponting's Australians became only the sixth side in Test history to win after a first-innings deficit of more than 200 runs.

I stood on-field again in the third and final Test at the Bellerive Oval in Hobart, where I was treated to a little drama and a fine batting display by some of the Australian batsmen. Most notably of these was Ricky Ponting, who was due for a big score. Before the Test, some cricketing 'experts' had advised him to eliminate his hook and pull shots. And his heart must have skipped a beat or two when, with his score on nought, he hooked a ball straight down the throat of young Aamer – who inexplicably spilt it. How Ponting made them pay! On 24, he was hit on the helmet attempting another hook and blood trickled from his right ear. Right up until he reached his 50, Ponting looked uncomfortable.

But once he got past 50, he delighted the crowd with some lovely cover drives and hook and pull shots, going on to score his 39th century and, eventually, a double century in Australia's first-innings total of 519. When he and Michael Clarke came together, the score read 71/3 – when Clarke was eventually out, Australia stood on 423/4, a partnership of 352 runs, of which Clarke contributed his best Test score to date (166). What better time for Ponting to come good than in front of his Tasmanian home crowd, which included his parents and the Australian prime minister.

The Aussies just kept on outplaying Pakistan and removed them for 301 (Salman Butt got a century). Instead of enforcing the follow-on, Ponting decided to bat again, and when he declared on 219/5, he had scored 89 and opener Simon Katich 100. Pakistan had all the time in the world to reach the required target, but it proved to be well beyond them. They were all out for 203. One can only speculate what would have happened had young Aamer held on to the catch from Ponting when he had zero, but those things happen in cricket. With victory in the third Test, Australia took the series 3-0.

Predictably, Ponting was voted Man of the Match, averaging 149 per innings, while Shane Watson was voted Player of the Series. Their performances will give Australia a lot of confidence for the year ahead; their skipper was back in top form, their best batsmen – Clarke, Watson, Katich and Hussey – were scoring plenty of runs, and spinner Nathan Hauritz (who took six wickets in the third Test and had a knock of 75) had a great series.

My last Test outing was in Hamilton, where New Zealand hosted Bangladesh. The standout performances here were Martin Guptill's marathon innings of 189, scored off 310 balls, and Brendon McCullum's 185 off 272 balls. This allowed the Kiwis to declare at 553 for seven.

Bangladesh responded not too badly, scoring 408 all out, with Mohammad Mahmudullah contributing 115 before being trapped lbw by Daniel Vettori. In their second innings, New Zealand declared at 258 for five, leaving Bangladesh a target of 404 runs. Despite 100 runs by Shakib Al Hasan, it proved too much for the Bangladeshis and they were all out for 282.

There was not much rest for me, as I had to fly off to the 2010 IPL tournament, after which I was scheduled to go to the West Indies for the Twenty20 Championship. The IPL was marked not only by consistent great performances by Sachin Tendulkar and Jacques Kallis, but also by the resignation of Indian minister Shashi Tharoor and reports of various government agencies investigating the IPL's financial transactions. Media reports at the time also suggested that the Indian Corporate Affairs ministry was planning to investigate the manner in which the IPL franchises are run.

At the time of writing, I still have the exciting Twenty20 tournament in the West Indies to look forward to, and will have to wait and see what the rest of the 2010 season holds in store for me. I have been a member of the Emirates Elite Panel since its inception in April 2002, and I've been fortunate to have been involved up to now.

The ICC is committed to the ongoing development of all international officials, and in June 2008 appointed five regional umpires' performance managers (UPMs), who are brought together for training annually. A full-time digital video specialist is also employed to help review decisions, and the UPMs conduct regular reviews in Dubai as they pass through on assignment. The composition of the panel is reviewed by the ICC every year and announced on 1 April, as it will be again in 2010.

I would like to mention that, on average, an umpire on the Emirates Elite Panel stands in eight to 10 Test matches and 10 to 15 ODIs annually, as well as in any ICC events scheduled for that year, for example a World Cup or a championship. That means a potential on-field workload of 75 days; include travel and time to prepare, and it runs into quite a few days per year! Personally I feel the old body still has a few years of umpiring left in it, and I would like to go on until at least the 2011 World Cup. As mentioned before, I still haven't stood on-field in a World Cup final, which I would dearly love to do. Whatever happens, at the end of the day I will be able to look back on a wonderful time spent in a wonderful sport.

The game has been good to me, and I hope I have given enough in return.

RUDI KOERTZEN'S MATCHES AS ON-FIELD UMPIRE
Test matches, 1992–2010

MATCH	GROUND	START DATE
South Africa vs India	Port Elizabeth	26 Dec 1992
South Africa vs India	Cape Town	2 Jan 1997
South Africa vs Australia	Port Elizabeth	14 Mar 1997
Sri Lanka vs India	Colombo (SSC)	9 Aug 1997
South Africa vs Pakistan	Port Elizabeth	6 Mar 1998
South Africa vs Sri Lanka	Centurion	27 Mar 1998
Sri Lanka vs New Zealand	Colombo (RPS)	27 May 1998
Zimbabwe vs India	Harare	7 Oct 1998
South Africa vs West Indies	Port Elizabeth	10 Dec 1998
New Zealand vs India	Hamilton	2 Jan 1999
South Africa vs West Indies	Centurion	15 Jan 1999
Sri Lanka vs India	Colombo (SSC)	24 Feb 1999
Pakistan vs Sri Lanka	Lahore	4 Mar 1999
England vs New Zealand	Lord's	22 Jul 1999
India vs New Zealand	Ahmedabad	29 Oct 1999
South Africa vs England	Port Elizabeth	9 Dec 1999
South Africa vs England	Centurion	14 Jan 2000
West Indies vs Pakistan	Georgetown	5 May 2000
West Indies vs Pakistan	Bridgetown	18 May 2000
South Africa vs New Zealand	Port Elizabeth	30 Nov 2000
Australia vs West Indies	Sydney	2 Jan 2001
South Africa vs Sri Lanka	Centurion	20 Jan 2001
Sri Lanka vs England	Kandy	7 Mar 2001

India vs Australia	Chennai	18 Mar 2001
Zimbabwe vs Bangladesh	Bulawayo	19 Apr 2001
England vs Australia	The Oval	23 Aug 2001
Sri Lanka vs Bangladesh	Colombo (SSC)	6 Sep 2001
South Africa vs Australia	Johannesburg	22 Feb 2002
South Africa vs Australia	Cape Town	8 Mar 2002
Pakistan vs New Zealand	Lahore	1 May 2002
West Indies vs New Zealand	Bridgetown	21 Jun 2002
West Indies vs New Zealand	St George's	28 Jun 2002
England vs India	Lord's	25 Jul 2002
England vs India	Nottingham	8 Aug 2002
Australia vs England	Brisbane	7 Nov 2002
Australia vs England	Adelaide	21 Nov 2002
Australia vs England	Perth	29 Nov 2002
West Indies vs Australia	Georgetown	10 Apr 2003
West Indies vs Australia	Port of Spain	19 Apr 2003
Australia vs Bangladesh	Darwin	18 Jul 2003
Australia vs Bangladesh	Cairns	25 Jul 2003
India vs New Zealand	Ahmedabad	8 Oct 2003
India vs New Zealand	Mohali	16 Oct 2003
Zimbabwe vs West Indies	Bulawayo	12 Nov 2003
Australia vs India	Brisbane	4 Dec 2003
Australia vs India	Adelaide	12 Dec 2003
Sri Lanka vs Australia	Galle	8 Mar 2004
West Indies vs England	Bridgetown	1 Apr 2004
Pakistan vs India	Rawalpindi	13 Apr 2004
Zimbabwe vs Sri Lanka	Harare	6 May 2004
Zimbabwe vs Sri Lanka	Bulawayo	14 May 2004

England vs New Zealand	Lord's	20 May 2004
West Indies vs Bangladesh	Kingston	4 Jun 2004
England vs West Indies	Lord's	22 Jul 2004
England vs West Indies	The Oval	19 Aug 2004
India vs Australia	Chennai	14 Oct 2004
India vs Australia	Mumbai	3 Nov 2004
Australia vs Pakistan	Perth	16 Dec 2004
Australia vs Pakistan	Melbourne	26 Dec 2004
India vs Pakistan	Mohali	8 Mar 2005
New Zealand vs Australia	Wellington	18 Mar 2005
New Zealand vs Australia	Auckland	26 Mar 2005
England vs Australia	Lord's	21 Jul 2005
England vs Australia	Birmingham	4 Aug 2005
England vs Australia	The Oval	8 Sep 2005
Australia vs ICC World XI	Sydney	14 Oct 2005
Australia vs West Indies	Brisbane	3 Nov 2005
Australia vs West Indies	Hobart	17 Nov 2005
Pakistan vs England	Lahore	29 Nov 2005
Pakistan vs India	Lahore	13 Jan 2006
Pakistan vs India	Faisalabad	21 Jan 2006
New Zealand vs West Indies	Auckland	9 Mar 2006
Sri Lanka vs Pakistan	Colombo (SSC)	26 Mar 2006
England vs Sri Lanka	Lord's	11 May 2006
England vs Sri Lanka	Nottingham	2 Jun 2006
West Indies vs India	Basseterre	22 Jun 2006
West Indies vs India	Kingston	30 Jun 2006
Australia vs England	Adelaide	1 Dec 2006
Australia vs England	Perth	14 Dec 2006

Australia vs England	Melbourne	26 Dec 2006
England vs West Indies	Lord's	17 May 2007
England vs West Indies	Leeds	25 May 2007
Sri Lanka vs Bangladesh	Colombo (PSS)	3 Jul 2007
Sri Lanka vs Bangladesh	Kandy	11 Jul 2007
Australia vs Sri Lanka	Brisbane	8 Nov 2007
Australia vs Sri Lanka	Hobart	16 Nov 2007
India vs Pakistan	Kolkata	30 Nov 2007
India vs Pakistan	Bangalore	8 Dec 2007
New Zealand vs England	Wellington	13 Mar 2008
New Zealand vs England	Napier	22 Mar 2008
Sri Lanka vs India	Galle	31 Jul 2008
Sri Lanka vs India	Colombo (PSS)	8 Aug 2008
India vs Australia	Bangalore	9 Oct 2008
India vs Australia	Mohali	17 Oct 2008
Australia vs New Zealand	Brisbane	20 Nov 2008
Australia vs New Zealand	Adelaide	28 Nov 2008
New Zealand vs West Indies	Napier	19 Dec 2008
West Indies vs England	Kingston	4 Feb 2009
West Indies vs England	St John's	15 Feb 2009
England vs Australia	Lord's	16 Jul 2009
England vs Australia	Birmingham	30 Jul 2009
New Zealand vs Pakistan	Wellington	3 Dec 2009
New Zealand vs Pakistan	Napier	11 Dec 2009
Australia vs Pakistan	Melbourne	26 Dec 2009
Australia vs Pakistan	Hobart	14 Jan 2010
New Zealand vs Bangladesh	Hamilton	15 Feb 2010

One Day Internationals, 1992–2010

MATCH	GROUND	START DATE
South Africa vs India	Port Elizabeth	9 Dec 1992
South Africa vs India	Bloemfontein	15 Dec 1992
South Africa vs India	East London	19 Dec 1992
South Africa vs West Indies	Port Elizabeth	11 Feb 1993
South Africa vs West Indies	Cape Town	17 Feb 1993
South Africa vs Pakistan	Centurion	21 Feb 1993
South Africa vs Australia	Port Elizabeth	22 Feb 1994
South Africa vs Australia	East London	2 Apr 1994
South Africa vs Australia	Cape Town	6 Apr 1994
Pakistan vs Sri Lanka	Centurion	4 Dec 1994
New Zealand vs Sri Lanka	Bloemfontein	8 Dec 1994
New Zealand vs Pakistan	Port Elizabeth	13 Dec 1994
South Africa vs Sri Lanka	Port Elizabeth	21 Dec 1994
South Africa vs England	Bloemfontein	11 Jan 1996
South Africa vs England	Johannesburg	13 Jan 1996
South Africa vs England	Port Elizabeth	21 Jan 1996
India vs Zimbabwe	Paarl	27 Jan 1997
South Africa vs Zimbabwe	Cape Town	29 Jan 1997
South Africa vs India	Port Elizabeth	2 Feb 1997
South Africa vs India	Durban	12 Feb 1997
South Africa vs India	Durban	13 Feb 1997
South Africa vs Australia	Port Elizabeth	31 Mar 1997
South Africa vs Australia	Cape Town	2 Apr 1997
South Africa vs Australia	Bloemfontein	13 Apr 1997
India vs Pakistan	Toronto	13 Sep 1997

India vs Pakistan	Toronto	17 Sep 1997
India vs Pakistan	Toronto	18 Sep 1997
India vs Pakistan	Toronto	20 Sep 1997
Kenya vs Bangladesh	Nairobi (Gym)	10 Oct 1997
Bangladesh vs Zimbabwe	Nairobi (Gym)	11 Oct 1997
Bangladesh vs Zimbabwe	Nairobi (Aga)	14 Oct 1997
Kenya vs Bangladesh	Nairobi (Aga)	15 Oct 1997
Kenya vs Zimbabwe	Nairobi (Aga)	16 Oct 1997
Kenya vs Zimbabwe	Nairobi (Gym)	18 Oct 1997
Kenya vs Zimbabwe	Nairobi (Gym)	19 Oct 1997
India vs Pakistan	Dhaka	11 Jan 1998
Bangladesh vs Pakistan	Dhaka	12 Jan 1998
India vs Pakistan	Dhaka	16 Jan 1998
India vs Pakistan	Dhaka	18 Jan 1998
Pakistan vs Sri Lanka	Kimberley	7 Apr 1998
South Africa vs Sri Lanka	Port Elizabeth	13 Apr 1998
South Africa vs Pakistan	Centurion	17 Apr 1998
South Africa vs Pakistan	Cape Town	23 Apr 1998
South Africa vs West Indies	East London	24 Jan 1999
South Africa vs West Indies	Port Elizabeth	30 Jan 1999
South Africa vs West Indies	Cape Town	2 Feb 1999
England vs Sri Lanka	Lord's	14 May 1999
England vs Kenya	Canterbury	18 May 1999
Australia vs Pakistan	Leeds	23 May 1999
New Zealand vs Pakistan	Derby	28 May 1999
Scotland vs New Zealand	Edinburgh	31 May 1999
Australia vs Zimbabwe	Lord's	9 Jun 1999
India vs Zimbabwe	Singapore	4 Sep 1999

India vs West Indies	Singapore	5 Sep 1999
India vs West Indies	Singapore	7 Sep 1999
India vs West Indies	Singapore	8 Sep 1999
South Africa vs England	Cape Town	26 Jan 2000
South Africa vs England	East London	4 Feb 2000
South Africa vs Zimbabwe	Port Elizabeth	6 Feb 2000
South Africa vs England	Johannesburg	13 Feb 2000
South Africa vs Australia	Cape Town	14 Apr 2000
South Africa vs Australia	Johannesburg	16 Apr 2000
South Africa vs New Zealand	Potchefstroom	20 Oct 2000
South Africa vs New Zealand	Benoni	22 Oct 2000
South Africa vs New Zealand	Kimberley	28 Oct 2000
South Africa vs New Zealand	Cape Town	4 Nov 2000
South Africa vs Sri Lanka	Port Elizabeth	15 Dec 2000
South Africa vs Sri Lanka	Cape Town	11 Jan 2001
South Africa vs Sri Lanka	Bloemfontein	14 Jan 2001
South Africa vs India	Johannesburg	5 Oct 2001
South Africa vs Kenya	Benoni	7 Oct 2001
South Africa vs India	East London	19 Oct 2001
South Africa vs Kenya	Cape Town	22 Oct 2001
Sri Lanka vs Zimbabwe	Sharjah	26 Oct 2001
Pakistan vs Sri Lanka	Sharjah	27 Oct 2001
Sri Lanka vs Zimbabwe	Sharjah	30 Oct 2001
Pakistan vs Zimbabwe	Sharjah	31 Oct 2001
Pakistan vs Sri Lanka	Sharjah	4 Nov 2001
South Africa vs Australia	Potchefstroom	27 Mar 2002
South Africa vs Australia	Durban	3 Apr 2002
West Indies vs New Zealand	Gros Islet	8 Jun 2002

West Indies vs New Zealand	Port of Spain	12 Jun 2002
Kenya vs Pakistan	Nairobi (Gym)	29 Aug 2002
Kenya vs Pakistan	Nairobi (Gym)	1 Sep 2002
Australia vs Pakistan	Nairobi (Gym)	4 Sep 2002
India vs Zimbabwe	Colombo (RPS)	14 Sep 2002
England vs Zimbabwe	Colombo (RPS)	18 Sep 2002
Netherlands vs Pakistan	Colombo (SSC)	21 Sep 2002
Australia vs England	Sydney	13 Dec 2002
England vs Sri Lanka	Brisbane	17 Dec 2002
Australia vs Sri Lanka	Perth	22 Dec 2002
New Zealand vs West Indies	Port Elizabeth	13 Feb 2003
England vs Netherlands	East London	16 Feb 2003
Zimbabwe vs India	Harare	19 Feb 2003
England vs Pakistan	Cape Town	22 Feb 2003
England vs India	Durban	26 Feb 2003
India vs Pakistan	Centurion	1 Mar 2003
New Zealand vs Zimbabwe	Bloemfontein	8 Mar 2003
Sri Lanka vs Zimbabwe	East London	15 Mar 2003
Australia vs Sri Lanka	Port Elizabeth	18 Mar 2003
West Indies vs Australia	Port of Spain	24 May 2003
West Indies vs Australia	Port of Spain	25 May 2003
West Indies vs Australia	St George's	30 May 2003
West Indies vs Australia	St George's	1 Jun 2003
Zimbabwe vs West Indies	Bulawayo	22 Nov 2003
Zimbabwe vs West Indies	Bulawayo	23 Nov 2003
Australia vs Zimbabwe	Sydney	11 Jan 2004
Australia vs Zimbabwe	Hobart	16 Jan 2004
India vs Zimbabwe	Brisbane	20 Jan 2004

India vs Zimbabwe	Adelaide	24 Jan 2004
Australia vs Zimbabwe	Melbourne	29 Jan 2004
India vs Zimbabwe	Perth	3 Feb 2004
Australia vs India	Sydney	8 Feb 2004
New Zealand vs West Indies	Birmingham	26 Jun 2004
England vs New Zealand	Chester-le-Street	29 Jun 2004
New Zealand vs West Indies	Cardiff	3 Jul 2004
England vs West Indies	Lord's	6 Jul 2004
New Zealand vs West Indies	Lord's	10 Jul 2004
India vs Kenya	Southampton	11 Sep 2004
Australia vs New Zealand	The Oval	16 Sep 2004
India vs Pakistan	Birmingham	19 Sep 2004
England vs Australia	Birmingham	21 Sep 2004
England vs West Indies	The Oval	25 Sep 2004
Australia vs New Zealand	Melbourne (Dock)	5 Dec 2004
Australia vs New Zealand	Sydney	8 Dec 2004
Asia XI vs ICC World XI	Melbourne	10 Jan 2005
Australia vs West Indies	Melbourne	14 Jan 2005
Pakistan vs West Indies	Brisbane	19 Jan 2005
Australia vs Pakistan	Sydney	23 Jan 2005
Pakistan vs West Indies	Adelaide	28 Jan 2005
Pakistan vs West Indies	Perth	1 Feb 2005
Australia vs Pakistan	Sydney	6 Feb 2005
India vs Pakistan	Ahmedabad	12 Apr 2005
India vs Pakistan	Kanpur	15 Apr 2005
India vs Pakistan	Delhi	17 Apr 2005
England vs Australia	Leeds	7 Jul 2005
England vs Australia	Lord's	10 Jul 2005

England vs Australia	The Oval	12 Jul 2005
Australia vs ICC World XI	Melbourne (Dock)	7 Oct 2005
Pakistan vs England	Karachi	15 Dec 2005
Pakistan vs England	Rawalpindi	19 Dec 2005
Pakistan vs England	Rawalpindi	21 Dec 2005
New Zealand vs West Indies	Wellington	18 Feb 2006
New Zealand vs West Indies	Queenstown	22 Feb 2006
New Zealand vs West Indies	Christchurch	25 Feb 2006
New Zealand vs West Indies	Napier	1 Mar 2006
India vs England	Kochi	6 Apr 2006
India vs England	Jamshedpur	12 Apr 2006
India vs England	Indore	15 Apr 2006
India vs Pakistan	Abu Dhabi	18 Apr 2006
India vs Pakistan	Abu Dhabi	19 Apr 2006
West Indies vs Zimbabwe	Ahmedabad	8 Oct 2006
Sri Lanka vs West Indies	Mumbai (BS)	14 Oct 2006
Australia vs West Indies	Mumbai (BS)	18 Oct 2006
New Zealand vs Sri Lanka	Mumbai (BS)	20 Oct 2006
New Zealand vs Pakistan	Mohali	25 Oct 2006
Australia vs New Zealand	Mohali	1 Nov 2006
Australia vs West Indies	Mumbai (BS)	5 Nov 2006
South Africa vs Pakistan	Centurion	4 Feb 2007
South Africa vs Pakistan	Port Elizabeth	9 Feb 2007
South Africa vs Pakistan	Johannesburg	14 Feb 2007
Bangladesh vs Bermuda	St John's	25 Feb 2007
Bermuda vs Canada	St John's	26 Feb 2007
Bangladesh vs Canada	St John's	28 Feb 2007
England vs New Zealand	Gros Islet	16 Mar 2007

Kenya vs New Zealand	Gros Islet	20 Mar 2007
England vs Kenya	Gros Islet	24 Mar 2007
West Indies vs New Zealand	North Sound	29 Mar 2007
Bangladesh vs New Zealand	North Sound	2 Apr 2007
Australia vs England	North Sound	8 Apr 2007
Australia vs Ireland	Bridgetown	13 Apr 2007
West Indies vs Bangladesh	Bridgetown	19 Apr 2007
West Indies vs England	Bridgetown	21 Apr 2007
New Zealand vs Sri Lanka	Kingston	24 Apr 2007
Sri Lanka vs Bangladesh	Colombo (PSS)	20 Jul 2007
Sri Lanka vs Bangladesh	Colombo (RPS)	23 Jul 2007
Sri Lanka vs Bangladesh	Colombo (RPS)	25 Jul 2007
Sri Lanka vs England	Dambulla	1 Oct 2007
Sri Lanka vs England	Dambulla	4 Oct 2007
Sri Lanka vs England	Dambulla	7 Oct 2007
Sri Lanka vs England	Colombo (RPS)	10 Oct 2007
Sri Lanka vs England	Colombo (RPS)	13 Oct 2007
South Africa vs West Indies	Centurion	20 Jan 2008
Australia vs India	Brisbane	3 Feb 2008
India vs Sri Lanka	Brisbane	5 Feb 2008
Australia vs India	Melbourne	10 Feb 2008
Australia vs Sri Lanka	Perth	15 Feb 2008
Australia vs Sri Lanka	Melbourne	22 Feb 2008
India vs Sri Lanka	Hobart	26 Feb 2008
Australia vs India	Sydney	2 Mar 2008
New Zealand vs India	Napier	3 Mar 2009
New Zealand vs India	Wellington	6 Mar 2009
New Zealand vs India	Christchurch	8 Mar 2009

New Zealand vs India	Hamilton	11 Mar 2009
New Zealand vs India	Auckland	14 Mar 2009
South Africa vs Australia	Durban	3 Apr 2009
South Africa vs Australia	Cape Town	9 Apr 2009
South Africa vs Australia	Johannesburg	17 Apr 2009
Ireland vs Kenya	Dublin	9 Jul 2009
Ireland vs Kenya	Dublin	11 Jul 2009
Ireland vs Kenya	Dublin	12 Jul 2009
South Africa vs Zimbabwe	Benoni	8 Nov 2009
New Zealand vs Australia	Napier	3 Mar 2010
New Zealand vs Australia	Auckland	6 Mar 2010

Twenty20 matches, 2007–2009

MATCH	GROUND	START DATE
South Africa vs Pakistan	Johannesburg	2 Feb 2007
South Africa vs West Indies	Johannesburg	18 Jan 2008
South Africa vs Australia	Johannesburg	27 Mar 2009
Pakistan vs Sri Lanka	Lord's	12 Jun 2009
India vs West Indies	Lord's	12 Jun 2009
Ireland vs Pakistan	The Oval	15 Jun 2009
England vs West Indies	The Oval	15 Jun 2009
Sri Lanka vs West Indies	The Oval	19 Jun 2009

Bibliography

BOOKS

Magazine, Pradeep. *Not Quite Cricket*. Penguin, 2000.

Oosthuizen, A, and G Tinkler. *The Banjo Players: Cricket's Match Fixing Scandal*. Riverside Publications, 2001.

Procter, Mike. *South Africa: The Years of Isolation and the Return to International Cricket*. Queen Anne Press, 1994.

Wilde, Simon. *Caught: The Full Story of Corruption in International Cricket*. Aurum Press, 2001.

NEWSPAPERS

Die Burger, 1989–2009

WEBSITES

cricinfo.com

stgeorgespark.nmmu.ac.za

wikipedia.org

telegraph.co.uk

theaustralian.news.com

Index

DRS (decision review system) 47, 146,
147, 148, 187, 190
Duckworth-Lewis method 98, 105,
112, 119

Eastern Province (cricket team) 8, 15,
20, 21
Eastern Province (rugby team) 12
Eastern Province Umpires
Association 20
Eden Gardens (Kolkata) 27
Edgbaston (Birmingham) 74, 75, 78,
91, 92, 93, 97
Edwards, Fidel 65, 67
Eksteen, Clive 26
Elite Panel of Umpires 46, 138,
201, 202
Emerson, Ross 162
England 33, 34, 37, 38, 39, 40, 43,
44, 48, 49–50, 56, 57, 60, 62, 66,
68, 69–81, 83–93, 97, 98, 100,
101, 102, 104, 108, 109, 110,
116, 117, 179, 183
Erasmus, Rassie 6
Estwick, Rod 179, 180

Farbrace, Paul 180
Farhat, Imran 198
Ferreira, Anton 182
FICA (Federation of International
Cricketers' Associations) 194
Fleming, Stephen 178
Flintoff, Andrew 53, 74, 75–76, 77,
78, 79, 84, 85, 89, 90, 91, 116,
144, 157, 158–159, 173, 192
Flower, Andy 147, 148
Flower, Grant 35
food poisoning 183–184
Forde, Keith 136
Free State (cricket team) 8, 21–23
Free State Cheetahs 6

Gaddafi Stadium (Lahore) 36
Gambhir, Gautam 64

Ganga, Daren 57
Ganguly, Sourav 33, 37, 62
Gatting, Mike 26, 78, 161
Gavaskar, Sunil 36, 72
Gayle, Chris 65, 66, 67, 97, 107, 108,
156–157
Gerber, Danie 6
Ghauri, Nadeem 180
Gibbs, Herschelle 80, 106, 111, 116,
125, 126, 166
Gilchrist, Adam 46, 52, 61, 65, 71, 73,
76, 87, 98, 102, 103, 104, 105,
111, 112, 113, 118, 155–156, 170
Giles, Ashley 76, 85
Gillespie, Jason 33, 72, 76
Gooch, Graham 25
Gough, Darren 100, 101
Greig, Tony 70
Grey High School 11, 15
Griqualand West 18
Guptill, Martin 201

Haddin, Brad 65, 89, 90, 91
Hadlee, Richard 72
Hair, Darrell 39, 52, 56, 57–60, 84,
127, 140, 162, 175
Hall, Andrew 194
Hall, Wes 67
Hammond, Wally 17, 33, 84
Harare Sports Club 35
Harmison, Steve 66, 74, 77, 85, 144
Harper, Daryl 67, 68, 135, 138, 172
Hauritz, Nathan 145, 199, 201
Hawk-Eye 133–134, 139, 141,
146, 148
Hayden, Matthew 32, 45, 46, 51, 64,
72, 74, 76, 79, 85, 87, 117, 118,
153–154
Hayward, Nantie 102
Headingley (Leeds) 92
Henry, Omar 19
Hill, Tony 67, 68, 144, 147
Hinds, Wavell 41, 103
Hirwani, Narendra 45

Hogg, Brad 117
Hoggard, Matthew 84, 85, 87
Hot Spot 142, 143–144, 146, 47–148
Howell, David 15
Howell, Eddie 15
Howell, Ian 15
Hudson, Andrew 26, 98
Hughes, Kim 11, 26
Hughes, Merv 32
Hughes, Phillip 89, 90, 145
Hurst, Alan 66, 67
Hurter, Karl 136
Hussain, Nasser 38, 39, 44, 48,
    128, 129
Hussey, Mike 53, 60, 85, 87, 90, 91,
    92, 93, 105, 199, 201
Hutton, Len 17

ICC 2, 38, 46–47, 51, 56–60, 63, 65,
    96, 106, 118, 120–122, 129, 132,
    135, 137, 140, 141, 142, 144, 147,
    162, 172, 176, 180, 195, 201–202
ICL 131, 132, 193–194
India 29–31, 32, 36, 37, 43, 45, 48,
    49, 50, 52, 55, 56, 59, 60, 62, 63,
    88, 97, 100, 101, 103, 104, 105,
    113, 116, 130, 179, 189, 193
Indian Cricket League see ICL
Indian Premier League see IPL
International Cricket Council see ICC
international isolation of SA cricket
    ban (1970) 1, 13, 30, 36
    readmission (1991) 1, 13, 27
Inzamam-ul-Haq 47, 52, 56, 103,
    116, 140, 166
IPL 107–108, 131, 132, 158, 188,
    192–195, 201
Ireland 96, 112, 116

Jadeja, Ajay 126
Jaffer, Wasim 57, 62
Jaques, Phil 60–61
Jayaprakash, Arani 179
Jayasuriya, Sanath 33, 44, 118, 155

Jayawardene, Mahela 33, 36, 63, 119,
    141, 155, 174
Jerling, Brian 7
Johnson, Martin 6
Johnson, Mel 176
Johnson, Mitchell 90, 92, 93, 199
Johnson, Neil 110
Jones, Dean 99
Jones, Geraint 74, 77
Jones, Simon 77
Justice Qayyum Report 125

Kallicharran, Alvin 8, 21, 22, 23, 184
Kallis, Jacques ix–x, 36, 37–38, 52,
    136, 158, 189, 201
Kaneria, Danish 198, 199
Kasprowicz, Michael 77, 164
Katich, Simon 64, 74, 89, 198,
    200, 201
Kemp, Justin 194
Kenya 96, 111, 112
Khan, Younis 55, 62, 130
Khan, Zaheer 64, 142
Kieswetter, Craig 50
King, Judge Edwin 126
King Commission 126, 128
Kirsten, Gary 32, 34, 38
Kirsten, Peter 24, 29–30
Kiwis see New Zealand
Klusener, Lance 32, 35, 37, 39, 101,
    102, 112, 194
Knott, Alan 26
Koertzen, Eumelda [daughter] 2
Koertzen, Fonnie [sister] 5, 8
Koertzen, Hyla [wife] 2
Koertzen, Josef [father] 5, 8, 20
Koertzen, Luan [son] 2, 25, 177
Koertzen, Maria [mother] 5, 8, 20
Koertzen, Marie [sister] 5, 8, 20
Koertzen, Rudi
    'Slow Death' (nickname) ix, 3, 145
    milestones and achievements 1–2
    childhood and early adulthood 5–15
    as cricket player 10, 14–15, 18

Do you have any comments, suggestions or
feedback about this book or any other Zebra Press titles?
Contact us at **talkback@zebrapress.co.za**